Learning for Earning

Your Route to Success

by

John A. Wanat
Consultant and Author on Occupational Education
Jackson, New Jersey

E. Weston Pfeiffer
Consultant on Technical and Vocational Training
Lambertville, New Jersey

Richard Van Gulik, PhD
Assistant Director—Curriculum
Withlacoochee Technical Institute
Inverness, Florida

Publisher
The Goodheart-Willcox Company, Inc.
Tinley Park, Illinois
www.g-w.com

Introduction

This *Student Workbook* is designed for use with the text *Learning for Earning: Your Route to Success.* It will help you understand and remember the facts and concepts about career exploration presented in the text. It will also help you apply what you learn to your everyday life.

The activities in this workbook are divided into chapters that correspond to those in the text. By reading the text first, you will have the information needed to complete the activities. Try to complete them without referring to the text. Later, you can check the text to complete any answer you did not finish. At that time, you can also compare your answers to the information in the text.

Most of the *Workbook's* activities are designed to stimulate your thinking and help you apply the new information. These ask for your opinions and ideas, so there are no right or wrong answers. Other activities have right answers and can be used as review guides when you study for tests and quizzes. An example is the vocabulary exercise that begins each chapter. It uses a matching or fill-in-the-blank activity or a crossword puzzle to review the new terms introduced in the text.

Exploring careers is fun but, more importantly, it opens your eyes to the wide range of jobs in the workplace. *Learning for Earning* will help you identify the career that is best for you.

Manufactured in the United States of America.
ISBN 978-1-59070-948-1
2 3 4 5 6 7 8 9 – 09 – 14 13 12 11 10 09

Contents

Part One — Exploring the World of Work

Part Two — Exploring Career Options

Part Three — Making Plans for Career Success

Part Four — Acquiring Workplace Skills

Part Five — Developing Personal Skills for Job Success

Part Six — Managing Your Money

Part Seven — Growing Toward Independence

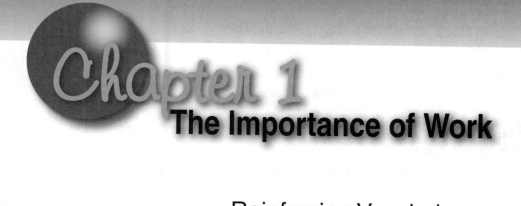

Chapter 1
The Importance of Work

Reinforcing Vocabulary

Activity A
Chapter 1

Name ______________________________
Date ____________________ **Period** __________

Match the following terms with their definitions.

_______ 1. An activity done to produce or accomplish something.
_______ 2. The work a person does, usually to earn money.
_______ 3. Employment that requires related skills and experiences.
_______ 4. A series of occupations, usually in the same or related fields, that helps you advance in a chosen field of work.
_______ 5. An illustration that shows a sequence of work in a career field, from entry to advanced levels.
_______ 6. The amount of money a person receives for doing a job.
_______ 7. The basics a person must have in order to live.
_______ 8. The items a person would like to have, but are not needed to survive.
_______ 9. The sum of traits that distinguishes a person as an individual.
_______ 10. A person's typical way of life.
_______ 11. The confidence a person has in himself or herself.
_______ 12. The way goods and services are produced, distributed, and consumed in a society.
_______ 13. The 16 broad groups of occupational and career specialties.
_______ 14. Skills used in one career that can be used in another.

A. career
B. career clusters
C. career ladder
D. economy
E. identity
F. income
G. job
H. lifestyle
I. needs
J. occupation
K. self-esteem
L. transferable skills
M. wants
N. work

Your Thoughts on Work

Activity B
Chapter 1

Name ______________________________
Date __________________ **Period** __________

Begin thinking about how your work will fit into your life. Do so by providing answers to the following questions. Then discuss your ideas in class.

1. You will probably have a job because you need income to live. List three other important reasons you will work.

   A. ______________________________

   B. ______________________________

   C. ______________________________

2. List three benefits you hope to gain from working.

   A. ______________________________

   B. ______________________________

   C. ______________________________

3. List five transferable skills you think are important to job success in any type of job.

   A. ______________________________

   B. ______________________________

   C. ______________________________

   D. ______________________________

   E. ______________________________

4. What type of work interests you? Why? ______________________________

5. What personal qualities would help you succeed in the type of work that interests you? __________

6. How would doing this type of work affect your lifestyle? ______________________________

Working to Help Others

Activity C
Chapter 1

Name ______________________________
Date ______________ **Period** __________

Throughout history, many people have chosen to do work that helps others. These people are often successful without making a lot of money. Success comes to them in the form of pride and satisfaction in helping others. Answer the following questions about people who work to help society.

1. Name three famous people, living or dead, who have contributed to others while living a simple lifestyle. Include a short statement of each person's accomplishments.

   A. ______________________________

   B. ______________________________

   C. ______________________________

2. Name three people you know personally who have contributed to others while living a simple lifestyle. Write a short statement of what each person has done.

   A. ______________________________

   B. ______________________________

   C. ______________________________

3. If you were given the chance to talk to any interesting person who works to help others, whom would you choose? Why? ______________________________

4. List three qualities that most people who help others have in common.

   A. ______________________________

   B. ______________________________

   C. ______________________________

5. What would you like to contribute to society during your own life? ______________________________

Careers That Meet Your Goals

Activity D **Name** ______________________
Chapter 1 **Date** ______________ **Period** ________

Whether you reach many of your goals in life will depend on the career you choose. List some of your goals related to each topic in the chart. Then list careers that you think would help you meet your goals.

	Your Goals	Careers to Help You Meet Your Goals
1. Income		
2. Identity		
3. Lifestyle		
4. Satisfaction		

Chapter 2
The Changing Workplace

Reinforcing Vocabulary

Activity A
Chapter 2

Name ____________________
Date ______________ **Period** __________

Match the following terms with their correct definitions.

_______ 1. An economy in which individuals and businesses play a major role in making decisions.
_______ 2. The money left in a business after all expenses are paid.
_______ 3. Goods and services created by companies in one country are sold to customers in other countries.
_______ 4. Nonmaterial assistance for which people are willing to pay.
_______ 5. Work programs that help employees to balance the demand of work and family.
_______ 6. A work schedule that permits flexibility in work hours.
_______ 7. Individuals who can take care of themselves; who can earn a salary that will support their needs and wants as well as those of their future families.
_______ 8. The characteristics or makeup of a population.
_______ 9. The positive result of people of different racial, ethnic, and cultural backgrounds working together.
_______ 10. The practice of one company contracting with another to handle work more efficiently and keep costs in line.
_______ 11. The application of scientific principles.
_______ 12. The total change in the way people live and work caused by computers.
_______ 13. Working at home through an electronic linkup with the central office.
_______ 14. The global computer linkup of individuals, groups, and organizations in government, business, and education.
_______ 15. Electronic retailing.
_______ 16. Electronic commerce.
_______ 17. Continually updating your knowledge and skills.

A. computer revolution
B. demographics
C. diversity
D. e-commerce
E. e-tailing
F. family-friendly programs
G. flextime
H. free enterprise system
I. global economy
J. Internet
K. lifelong learning
L. outsourcing
M. profit
N. self-sufficient
O. services
P. technology
Q. telecommuting

Workplace Solutions

Activity B **Name** ______________________________
Chapter 2 **Date** ________________ **Period** __________

Read the case study below and provide your solutions to the problems of Specialty Products Company.

Case Study

Specialty Products Company has hired you as a consultant. Their earnings have been decreasing in recent years. Your task is to provide the company management with recommendations to help turn the company around and become profitable again.

After six months of study, you have observed the following:

- Specialty Products Company has a high turnover rate among their employees, especially those who are young parents.
- Specialty Products Company only sells their products in the U.S.
- The methods and equipment that Specialty Products Company uses are the same as when they started their business in 1968.
- They spend a large part of their revenues on property landscaping and maintenance.
- The company's employees feel that management doesn't care about their ideas, many of which they feel could help the company operate more efficiently.

List below the recommendations you have for the management of Specialty Products Company. Give reasons for each of your recommendations.

Workforce Changes

Activity C
Chapter 2

Name ______________________
Date ______________ **Period** ________

Many factors are affecting the workforce today and will be in the future. Some of these are listed below. In the space provided, write your ideas of how the changes indicated might impact you and your career decisions.

Workplace Changes	How These Changes Might Impact Me and My Career Decisions
Social Change	
Population Shifts	
The Economy	
World Events	
Government Actions	
The Forces of Competition on Staff Size	

The Computer Revolution

Activity D **Name** ______________________

Chapter 2 **Date** ____________ **Period** ________

Computers have revolutionized the world of work. Briefly describe or give an example of how each form of technology listed below has affected the way people work.

Invention	How It Affects People Who Work
PC	
Laptops	
Telecommuting	
Internet	
E-tailing	
E-commerce	
Fiber-optics	
Global Positioning System (GPS)	

Chapter 3 The Law in the Workplace

Reinforcing Vocabulary

Activity A
Chapter 3

Name ______________________________
Date ____________________ **Period** ____________

In this chapter you learned about five government acts that were passed to protect workers' rights. These are listed below. Examples of discrimination relating to the workplace are also described. In the blank spaces below, write the letter of the act that addresses each action. Acts can be used more than once.

A. Age Discrimination Act
B. Americans with Disabilities Act
C. Equal Employment Opportunity Act
D. Equal Pay Act
E. Family and Medical Leave Act

_______ 1. Mark and Janis had waited many years to adopt a baby. Janis worked for a large ad agency. She was upset when her employer told her she couldn't have any time off from work to be with their new baby.

_______ 2. Jerome was surprised to see the following question on the job application: Do you have any disabilities?

_______ 3. Marisa and Jane were both up for a promotion. Both were equally qualified, but Jane got the job. Marisa felt that her race might have had something to do with the decision.

_______ 4. Ida had raised her children to adulthood. This past year, her husband of 30 years died. She decided to get a job, but the first place she applied turned her down. She was told that she was too old to learn to use a computer.

_______ 5. Maria discovered that Ben was being paid more for doing the very same job in their office even though they were hired at the same time.

_______ 6. Mr. Yung had worked 30 years for the Atlas Company when it was bought by another company. The new owners decided to cut payroll costs by letting the oldest employees go.

_______ 7. Caleb was told that the company had given the job to another applicant. He wondered if it was because he was Jewish.

_______ 8. Hector's father became gravely ill. He lived with Hector. Without Hector to care for him, he would have to be hospitalized. Hector asked his boss at the large manufacturing plant where he worked if he could take some time off to care for his father in the few weeks he had left to live. His boss turned him down.

_______ 9. Sheniqua had worked hard to get her college degree, but she looked very young. At the first place she applied, the manager said she was too young to be traveling and making sales calls on her own.

_______ 10. When Bonnie applied to work at ABC Auto Repair, the owner told her that he didn't hire women to work on cars. It was a man's job.

A Case of Discrimination

Activity B **Name** ______________________________
Chapter 3 **Date** ________________ **Period** __________

Read each of the cases described below and decide if discrimination might have occurred. Record your answers and solutions in the spaces provided.

Case I

Frank was promoted to the position of cashier. He worked in an entry position for 90 days before the promotion. Susan worked for the company full time for almost 18 months and is working as an assistant cashier. Susan believes she was discriminated against by their supervisor. She feels the promotion to the position of cashier should have been hers.

1. Do you think Susan has been discriminated against? ______________________________
2. What reasons might the employer have for promoting Frank rather than Susan? ______________
____
____
3. What would you tell Susan to do in this situation? ______________________________
____
____
4. What reason would Susan have for filing a discrimination complaint? ____________________
____
____

Case II

Mr. Rojaz was recently laid off from his job. He had worked for the company for 17 years. During that time, he had received five promotions, and he thought he was due for another one. Mr. Rojaz said he should have suspected the layoff because the company favors giving younger employees a chance. Most of his coworkers were also dismissed when they were about his age.

1. Do you think Mr. Rojaz has been discriminated against? ______________________________
2. What reasons might the employer have for letting Mr. Rojaz go? ______________________
____
____
3. What would you tell Mr. Rojaz to do in this situation? ______________________________
____
____
4. What reasons would Mr. Rojaz have for a discrimination complaint? ____________________
____
____

Is This Sexual Harassment?

Activity C
Chapter 3

Name ______________________________
Date ____________________ **Period** ____________

Read each of the statements given below. Decide whether the situation describes possible sexual harassment. Give the reasons for your conclusions.

1. "We have always had men and women working here. They always worked well together. We've always told jokes to each other. What's the big deal? Now that someone new is here, we can't tell jokes anymore?"

____

____

____

____

2. "Look, this is a body shop. Our suppliers provide us with the calendars. So some of them have naked models. So what? Is that a crime?"

____

____

____

____

3. "I was not talking to them. That conversation was between the two of us. How can that be harassment?"

____

____

____

____

4. "This has always been all women employees in this part of the company. He's a guy. How can we be sexually harassing him?"

____

____

____

____

5. "I don't like Mr. Jones. He's always on my case. I'm going to charge him with sexual harassment. That will fix him. Besides, what can happen to me?"

____

____

____

____

Taking Action

Activity D **Name** ______________________

Chapter 3 **Date** ______________ **Period** __________

Read the case study below. Then answer the questions that follow.

Case Study

Marsha began working for QTY Construction Company right after she graduated from high school. After attending an apprentice orientation meeting, she was sent to a construction site and assigned to a journey worker. The journey worker was to be her trainer for the first 1000 hours of the apprenticeship. When Marsha arrived at the job site, some of the journey workers began to kid her about being the only woman on the job. She was embarrassed by some of their comments, and she told them to stop. Several weeks passed and the comments continued. Then someone began leaving notes on her car.

Marsha told her trainer what was happening. He responded, "They give all the new apprentices the business. They just want to see if you can take it. I suggest you forget it if you want to complete this program. They're not doing anything different to you than to any other new worker. They were told to treat you just like one of the guys."

1. Do you think any law is being broken at this worksite? If so, what law? Give reasons for your answer.

2. What action should Marsha take at this point?

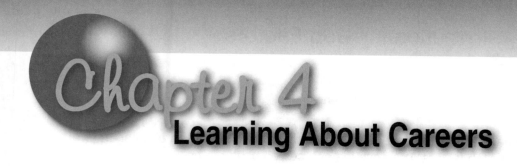

Chapter 4
Learning About Careers

Reinforcing Vocabulary

Activity A
Chapter 4

Name ________________________________
Date ____________________ **Period** __________

Use each of the terms or phrases listed below in a sentence that shows you understand the meaning of the term or phrase.

1. *traits*
   Sentence: ________________________________

2. *education*
   Sentence: ________________________________

3. *training*
   Sentence: ________________________________

4. *skills*
   Sentence: ________________________________

5. *entry-level jobs*
   Sentence: ________________________________

6. *advanced training*
   Sentence: ________________________________

7. *internship*
   Sentence: ________________________________

8. *promotion*
   Sentence: ________________________________

9. *fringe benefits*
   Sentence: ________________________________

10. *cost of living*
    Sentence: ________________________________

11. *job shadowing*
    Sentence: ________________________________

12. *cooperative education*
    Sentence: ________________________________

Investigating Job Factors

Activity B
Chapter 4

Name ______________________________
Date ____________________ **Period** ____________

Choose a career that is of interest to you. Using various resources described in this chapter, answer the following questions about basic job factors. Then cite the source you used to answer each question.

Career: ____

1. What are the main duties and responsibilities of this job? ______________________________

   ____

   ____

   ____

   ____

   Source: ____

2. What are the job prospects for this career? ______________________________

   ____

   ____

   ____

   Source: ____

3. What education, training, and skills are required for this job? ______________________________

   ____

   ____

   ____

   Source: ____

4. What is the typical starting salary for this job? ______________________________

   Source: ____

5. Is there opportunity for advancement in this career due to rapid growth in the field? Explain your answer. ______________________________

   Source: ____

6. Is this job available in most communities in this country? Explain your answer. ______________

   ____

   Source: ____

7. Describe the typical work environment for this job. ______________________________

   ____

   Source: ____

Obtaining Career Information

Activity C
Chapter 4

Name ____________________
Date ____________ **Period** ________

There are many ways to get the facts on jobs that interest you. Many of these ways are given below, but you need to supply the missing letters. Then complete each statement.

1. The __ * __ __ __ is a good place to start your career information search because ____________

2. The G __ __ __ __ for O __ __ __ __ __ __ __ __ __ __ __ Exploration is designed to help people ____________

3. A school C __ __ __ S __ __ __ __ can help you find out such information as ____________

4. If your computer is online, you can use the __ N __ __ __ N __ __ to find out such information as ____________

5. Public __ __ P __ __ Y __ __ __ __ services exist to help people ____________

6. By __ __ T __ __ __ __ __ W __ __ __ people who work in a field, you can learn ____________

7. J __ __ S __ __ __ __ __ __ __ __ even for a few days is enough time to ____________

8. By __ __ __ U __ T __ __ __ __ __ __ for community organizations you can ____________

9. One of the things you can learn from a __ __ __ __- __ I __ __ job is ____________

10. Schools often have __ A __ E __ __ days where they invite employers and other speakers to ____________

Getting to Know Career Information Sources

Activity D **Name** ______________________________
Chapter 4 **Date** _______________ **Period** __________

Visit your school or community library. See how many different types of sources of career information you can find there. You may ask a librarian for assistance. Describe each source below and then copy a sample of career information from each source.

1. Description of source:______________________________
   Sample of career information from this source: ______________________________
   ____
   ____
   ____
   ____
2. Description of source:______________________________
   Sample of career information from this source: ______________________________
   ____
   ____
   ____
   ____
3. Description of source:______________________________
   Sample of career information from this source: ______________________________
   ____
   ____
   ____
   ____
4. Description of source:______________________________
   Sample of career information from this source: ______________________________
   ____
   ____
   ____
   ____
5. Description of source:______________________________
   Sample of career information from this source: ______________________________
   ____
   ____
   ____
   ____

Chapter 5
Types of Careers

Reinforcing Vocabulary

Activity A **Name** ____________________
Chapter 5 **Date** ______________ **Period** ________

Match the following career clusters with their descriptions.

_____ 1. Careers that involve moving people and freight on land, at sea, and in the air.
_____ 2. Careers that include acting, writing, printing, and producing videos.
_____ 3. Careers that relate to working with plants, animals, food processing, and the environment.
_____ 4. Careers that relate to improving a person's quality of life.
_____ 5. Careers that involve production work in factories.
_____ 6. Careers that involve clerical, computer, accounting, management, and administrative work.
_____ 7. Careers that involve building and designing roads, bridges, and buildings.
_____ 8. Careers that involve the handling of money through banking, investing and accounting.
_____ 9. Careers that provide legislative, administrative, and regulatory services.
_____ 10. Careers that involve the promoting, buying, and selling of goods and services.
_____ 11. Careers that involve judicial, legal, and protective services.
_____ 12. Careers that involve making visitors happy.
_____ 13. Careers that involve designing, developing, managing, and supporting hardware and software information systems.
_____ 14. Careers that involve research as well as laboratory and testing services resulting in discoveries with the potential for improving life.
_____ 15. Careers that involve promoting health, wellness, and diagnosis as well as treating injuries and diseases.
_____ 16. Careers that involve training, guidance counseling, coaching, and library services.

A. Agriculture, Food, and Natural Resources
B. Architecture and Construction
C. Arts, Audio/Video Technology, and Communications
D. Business, Management, and Administration
E. Education and Training
F. Finance
G. Government and Public Administration
H. Health Science
I. Hospitality and Tourism
J. Human Services
K. Information Technology
L. Law, Public Safety, Corrections, and Security
M. Manufacturing
N. Marketing, Sales, and Service
O. Science, Technology, Engineering, and Mathematics
P. Transportation, Distribution, and Logistics

Occupational Research

Activity B **Name** ______________________
Chapter 5 **Date** ______________ **Period** ________

Select one occupation that interests you and answer the following questions about that occupation. Use the sources indicated to acquire information about it. Share the results of your research orally in class.

1. What is the title of an occupation that interests you? ______________________
2. Before consulting a resource, describe what you think people in this occupation do. ______________________
3. Consult career publications, Internet sites, videos, and CD-ROMs, and summarize their description of this occupation. ______________________
4. Where do people in this occupation work? ______________________
5. What is the general employment outlook for this occupation in five years? in 10 years? ______________________
6. How many people are employed in this occupation? ______________________
7. What local companies employ workers in this occupation? ______________________
8. In the following chart, list the major types of tools, equipment, machines, and materials used by workers in this occupation.

Tools	**Equipment**
Machines	**Materials**

(Continued)

Name ______________________________

9. Will you need training beyond high school for this occupation? __________ If so, what kind and amount of training will you need?

What Kind of Training?	How Much Training?
_____ On-the-job training _____ Apprenticeship _____ Trade or technical school _____ Community college _____ College or university _____ Military	

10. List qualifications other than education that are necessary in this occupation.

Physical Qualifications: ______________________________

____

____

Mental Qualifications: ______________________________

____

____

Emotional Qualifications: ______________________________

____

____

11. What are some similar occupations? ______________________________

____

12. Is the work dangerous? ______________________________

If so, in what way? ______________________________

____

What precautions do workers take to ensure their safety? ______________________________

____

____

13. Is the work seasonal? ______________________________

If so, when are peak employment periods? ______________________________

When are the off-seasons? ______________________________

Are layoffs common during off-seasons? ______________________________

14. Would you have to move from the area to be employed in this occupation? ______________________________

____

(Continued)

Name ______________________________

15. Compare your qualifications with the qualifications needed to work in this occupation.

My Qualifications	Required Qualifications

16. How can you develop any qualifications you are lacking? ______________________________

17. What have you learned about this occupation through job shadowing, career study tours, guest speakers, career fairs, and simulated work activities? ______________________________

18. Does this occupation still appeal to you? Explain. ______________________________

Exploring Career Clusters

Activity C
Chapter 5

Name ________________________
Date ______________ **Period** ________

The 16 career clusters described in this chapter are listed below. Place a check in front of the career clusters that interest you.

________ Agriculture, Food, and Natural Resources
________ Architecture and Construction
________ Arts, Audio/Video Technology, and Communications
________ Business, Management, and Administration
________ Education and Training
________ Finance
________ Government and Public Administration
________ Health Science
________ Hospitality and Tourism
________ Human Services
________ Information Technology
________ Law, Public Safety, Corrections, and Security
________ Manufacturing
________ Marketing, Sales, and Service
________ Science, Technology, Engineering, and Mathematics
________ Transportation, Distribution, and Logistics

In the space below, indicate the career clusters you checked and list at least two occupations for each cluster. Explain your interest in each occupation.

Name of cluster: ________________________
Occupations:
1. ________________________
2. ________________________
3. ________________________
4. ________________________

Reasons for your interest:
____
____
____
____

Name of cluster: ________________________
Occupations:
1. ________________________
2. ________________________
3. ________________________
4. ________________________

Reasons for your interest:
____
____
____
____

Name of cluster: ________________________
Occupations:
1. ________________________
2. ________________________
3. ________________________
4. ________________________

Reasons for your interest:
____
____
____
____

(Continued)

Name ______________________________

Name of cluster: ______________________

Occupations:

1. ______________________
2. ______________________
3. ______________________
4. ______________________

Reasons for your interest:

____
____
____
____

From all the occupations you listed, identify the two that interest you most.

Occupation 1: ______________________

Occupation 2: ______________________

List the abilities and skills needed for the occupations listed above.

Occupation 1: ______________________

Occupation 2: ______________________

Do you have the abilities and skills listed? What can you do to develop any abilities and skills you do not have?

Chapter 6
A Business of Your Own

Reinforcing Vocabulary

Activity A | **Name** ______________________
Chapter 6 | **Date** ____________ **Period** ________

Match the following terms with their correct definitions.

_______ 1. A business that can legally act as a single person, even though many people may own it.
_______ 2. A business that sells products.
_______ 3. Starting and owning a business of your own.
_______ 4. The easiest type of business to start and dissolve.
_______ 5. Someone who owns a share or shares of a corporation.
_______ 6. The right to sell a company's products in a specified area.
_______ 7. A type of business organization formed when two or more people combine their money and energy.
_______ 8. A business that performs tasks for customers.
_______ 9. Money needed to start and maintain a business.
_______ 10. A large quantity of items packaged in bulk with a per-item cost below the retail price.

A. corporation
B. entrepreneurship
C. franchise
D. partnership
E. retail
F. service
G. sole proprietorship
H. stockholder
I. wholesale
J. working capital

Retail and Service Businesses

Activity B **Name** ____________________
Chapter 6 **Date** __________ **Period** ________

Answer the following questions about retail and service businesses.

1. What kinds of retail businesses do you patronize? ____________________
2. List five retail businesses in your community and identify the types of products sold by each one.

	Business	Products
A.		
B.		
C.		
D.		
E.		

3. If you were starting a retail business, what kinds of products would you sell? ____________________
4. Why would you want to sell these kinds of products? ____________________
5. Why do you think people would want to buy these kinds of products? ____________________
6. List three franchise businesses in your community.
   A. ____________________
   B. ____________________
   C. ____________________
7. If you were starting a business, would you rather start a one-of-a-kind business or a franchise business? Explain. ____________________
8. What kinds of service businesses do you patronize? ____________________
9. List five service businesses in your community and identify the type of service provided by each.

	Business	Service
A.		
B.		
C.		
D.		
E.		

10. If you started a service business, what type of service would you like to provide? ____________________
11. Why would you want to provide this type of service? ____________________
12. Why do you think people would be willing to pay for your service? ____________________

Is Entrepreneurship for You?

Activity C
Chapter 6

Name ______________________________
Date ________________ **Period** __________

Answer the following questions to help determine if becoming an entrepreneur is a profession that appeals to you.

1. Which of the following goals do you have for your career? (Check all that apply.)

    _____ To make a lot of money.
    _____ To do your job better than another company or person.
    _____ To develop a new idea.
    _____ To be your own boss.
    _____ To set your own working hours.
    _____ To make your own decisions.
    _____ To gain recognition in the community.

2. Answer the following questions by checking either the Yes or No column.

	Yes	**No**
A. Do you have a good imagination?	_____	_____
B. Do you think you could manage a business successfully?	_____	_____
C. Do you often think of creative ways to solve problems?	_____	_____
D. Do you have a lot of ambition and drive?	_____	_____
E. Do you have a good knowledge of a product you would like to sell or a service you would like to provide?	_____	_____
F. Can you make decisions?	_____	_____
G. Can you supervise people well?	_____	_____
H. Can you motivate people to do their work well?	_____	_____
I. Are you comfortable around people you don't know?	_____	_____

3. Which of the following aspects of entrepreneurship would discourage you from starting your own business? (Check all that apply.)

    _____ long working hours
    _____ high level of stress
    _____ financial risk

4. What would you consider to be the biggest advantage of owning your own business? Explain.

    ____

    ____

5. What would you consider to be the biggest disadvantage of owning your own business? Explain.

    ____

    ____

6. Do you think you would like to be an entrepreneur? Explain. ______________________

    ____

    ____

Business Advice

Activity D
Chapter 6

Name ______________________

Date ______________ **Period** ________

Find out the answers to the questions below by inviting an entrepreneur to class or interviewing a friend or relative who is an independent businessperson.

Entrepreneur's name: ______________________

Type of business: ______________________

1. What kinds of products or services do you offer? ______________________
2. How long have you been in business? ______________________
3. What type of business organization do you have (sole proprietorship, partnership, or corporation)? Why did you choose that type of organization? ______________________
4. When did you first consider becoming an entrepreneur? ______________________
5. What was your main reason for wanting to start your own business? ______________________
6. Give a brief history of your business. ______________________
7. If you were starting over today, what would you do differently? ______________________
8. If you were starting over today, what would you do the same? ______________________
9. What is the biggest challenge of owning your own business? ______________________
10. What do you feel are the most important characteristics for an entrepreneur to have? ______________________
11. What advice would you offer to someone who is considering becoming an entrepreneur? ______________________

Planning a Business

Activity E
Chapter 6

Name ______________________
Date ____________ **Period** ________

You don't have to be an adult to be an entrepreneur! Complete this activity to plan a business you could start right now while in school.

1. What type of business do you want? ______________________
2. List any hobbies, classes, part-time jobs, or other accomplishments that provided you with some experience in this type of business. ______________________
____
3. What will you call your business? ______________________
4. Who will your customers be? (Consider age, sex, lifestyle, and any other characteristics that might encourage interest in your products or services.) ______________________
____
5. In the chart below, list all the equipment and supplies needed to start your business. Specify how many of each item you would need. For each item listed, check the appropriate column to indicate whether you would borrow it, buy it used, or buy it new. Estimate a cost for each item you would need to buy.

Item	Borrow	Buy Used	Buy New	Estimated Cost
			Total	

6. Can you run this business from your home? If not, where would you locate your business? ________
____
How much will it cost? ______________________
7. How will you advertise your business? ______________________
How much will it cost? ______________________
8. Can you run this business by yourself? ______________________
If not, who will help you? ______________________
____
How much will this cost? ______________________

(Continued)

Name ______________________________

9. Use the cost information from items 5 through 8 to estimate your total expenses for one week.

____

10. In the first column of the chart below, list the products or services that you believe will be your biggest moneymakers. In the second column, estimate how many of each product you will sell or how many times you will provide each service per week. In the third column, indicate how much you plan to charge for each product or service. Enter your total estimated income from each item in the last column. (Find this by multiplying the second and third columns for each item.)

Product or Service	Number per Week	Cost per Item	Income per Item
		Total Income per Week	

11. Subtract your estimate of total expenses per week (#9) from your estimate of total income per week (#10).
_______________ – _______________ = _______________

Will you make a profit or suffer a loss? _______________

12. Would you like to put this plan into action? Explain. _______________

Business Organizations

Activity F
Chapter 6

Name ____________________
Date ____________ **Period** ________

Use information from the chapter and library resources to investigate the different types of business organizations. Complete the chart below, listing the advantages and disadvantages of each type of organization. Then answer the questions that follow.

Type of Organization	Advantages	Disadvantages
Sole Proprietorship		
Partnership		
Corporation		

If you were starting a business, which type of business organization would you use? Explain.

____
____
____
____
____

(Continued)

Name ______________________________

Would you ever consider changing your business to another type of organization once it became successful? Explain.

Is there a type of business organization you definitely would not use? Explain.

Chapter 7
Learning About Yourself

Reinforcing Vocabulary

Activity A
Chapter 7

Name ______________________
Date ______________ **Period** __________

Match the following terms with the correct definitions. Also give examples where requested.

A. abilities
B. aptitudes
C. attitude
D. interests
E. personality
F. resources
G. self-concept
H. values

_______ 1. All the items or qualities you have or can use to help you get what you want.
Give two examples:
____
____

_______ 2. The group of traits that makes each person unique.
Name two common traits:
____
____

_______ 3. What you know and feel about yourself.

_______ 4. How you react to a situation.

_______ 5. Natural talents and the potential to learn easily and quickly.
Give two examples:
____
____

_______ 6. Skills you can develop and improve.
Give two examples:
____
____

_______ 7. Beliefs, ideas, or objects that are important to you.
Give two examples:
____
____

_______ 8. The ideas, subjects, or activities you enjoy.

Your Personality Traits and Self-Concept

Activity B **Name** ______________________________

Chapter 7 **Date** ____________________ **Period** __________

Personality traits are among the resources that can help you choose a career you will like. Evaluate your personality traits by placing a check in the blanks near the statements that describe you.

_________ 1. I like to work.
_________ 2. I am trustworthy.
_________ 3. I am often late to school.
_________ 4. I accept criticism and try to make improvements.
_________ 5. I am sure of myself.
_________ 6. I brag a lot.
_________ 7. I usually arrive at school early.
_________ 8. I am always willing to help others.
_________ 9. I only do things I like.
_________ 10. I am polite.
_________ 11. Before offering to help, I usually ask myself, "What's in it for me?"
_________ 12. I don't like being told what to do.
_________ 13. I am sometimes impolite.
_________ 14. I do only what I have to do to get along.
_________ 15. I like to work ahead.
_________ 16. I am almost always careful to do things right.
_________ 17. I am willing to work hard for what I want.
_________ 18. I need little direction to get jobs done.
_________ 19. I'd rather watch TV than go to school or work.
_________ 20. I believe telling a lie is sometimes better than telling the truth.
_________ 21. I don't believe I should have to work hard.
_________ 22. I'm often unsure of myself and my decisions.
_________ 23. I'm ambitious.
_________ 24. I'm often sloppy about my appearance.
_________ 25. I ignore things I don't like.
_________ 26. I like responsibility.
_________ 27. I like to please people.
_________ 28. I am almost always neat about my appearance.
_________ 29. I am often impatient with others.
_________ 30. I have trouble following directions.

From the list of traits you checked, identify the five that you believe are your best resources. Explain how each of these traits would be helpful in a career.

1. ____

2. ____

3. ____

4. ____

5. ____

(Continued)

Name ______________________________

Identify three traits you need to change—either positive traits you need to develop or negative traits you need to adjust. Explain why changing each of these traits would be helpful in a career.

1. ______________________________
2. ______________________________
3. ______________________________

Describe your self-concept.

____

Explain how your self-concept can affect your chances of getting and keeping a job.

____

Identifying My Interests—People, Data, Objects

Activity C
Chapter 7

Name ______________________
Date ______________ **Period** __________

To choose a career that you will enjoy, you must first know your interests. What do you like to do? Identify five activities you enjoy that focus on each of the following: people, data, and objects. Then answer the questions that follow.

People

Are you a "people" person? Do you like to join clubs, help others, give instructions, influence decisions, or plan social events? List five activities you enjoy that focus on people.

1. ______________________
2. ______________________
3. ______________________
4. ______________________
5. ______________________

Data (Ideas)

Are you a "data" person? Do you enjoy gathering information, working with numbers, maintaining records, and keeping track of details? List five activities you enjoy that focus on data.

1. ______________________
2. ______________________
3. ______________________
4. ______________________
5. ______________________

Objects (Things)

Are you a "things" person? Do you enjoy repairing items, operating machines, using tools, working on crafts, or gardening? List five activities you enjoy that focus on tools, machines, or other objects.

1. ______________________
2. ______________________
3. ______________________
4. ______________________
5. ______________________

(Continued)

Name ______________________________

Do your favorite interests focus on people, data, or objects? (If your favorite interests fall into two categories, name both.)______________________________

____

Of the 15 interests you listed on these two pages, which three do you enjoy most? List your favorite one first.

Interest #1:______________________________

Interest #2:______________________________

Interest #3:______________________________

What career possibilities relate to your three top interests?

Career(s) related to Interest #1:______________________________

____

Career(s) related to Interest #2:______________________________

____

Career(s) related to Interest #3:______________________________

____

Aptitudes, Abilities, and Values

Activity D
Chapter 7

Name ______________________________
Date ____________________ **Period** ____________

Define *aptitude*, *ability*, and *values* in the spaces provided. Then provide an example of one of the three qualities for each category listed below. Identify whether each example is an aptitude, ability, or value. The first example is provided for you.

Definitions

Aptitude:____

____

Ability: ____

____

Value:____

____

1. An example of a(n) value involving **family** is: eating dinners together every night to promote family unity and communication.
2. An example of a(n) ____________________ involving **public speaking** is:____________________
____
3. An example of a(n) ____________________ involving **education** is:____________________
____
4. An example of a(n) ____________________ involving **sports** is:____________________
____
5. An example of a(n) ____________________ involving a **musical instrument** is: ____________
____
6. An example of a(n) ____________________ involving **painting or some other fine art** is: ________
____
7. An example of a(n) ____________________ involving a **computer** is: ____________________
____
8. An example of a(n) ____________________ involving **science** is:____________________
____
9. An example of a(n) ____________________ involving **friends** is: ____________________
____
10. An example of a(n) ____________________ involving **time** is: ____________________
____

Chapter 8
Making Decisions

Reinforcing Vocabulary

Activity A
Chapter 8

Name ______________________________
Date ________________ **Period** ________

Read each of the definitions below and decide which chapter term is being defined. Write the correct term in the crossword puzzle.

Across

2. Personal decisions may also affect ______ decisions.
5. The ______-______ process is the seven-step guide for making choices based on careful thinking and planning.
8. A(n) ______ is a choice or option when making a decision.
9. After making a decision, it is important to ______ the results.
10. To ______ is to put a plan into action.

Down

1. A(n) ______ occurs when one thing is given up in return for another.
3. Decisions that are made often and automatically are ______ decisions.
4. The sixth step of the decision-making process is to develop a ______ of action.
5. The first step in making a decision is to ______ the decision to be made.
6. A decision that is made based on feelings or reactions to a situation is a(n) ______ decision.
7. Making a(n) ______ means making a choice or a judgment.

The Decision-Making Process

Activity B **Name** ______________________________

Chapter 8 **Date** _______________ **Period** __________

Match the following thoughts about deciding what to wear with the correct steps of the decision-making process. Then answer the questions that follow.

_______ 1. The sweater looks great on me, but I sometimes get too warm when I wear it. The flannel shirt looks old and faded. It also fits rather snugly. The sweatshirt looks casual, but neat. It is very comfortable.

_______ 2. I usually make good choices. I can listen to the weather forecast.

_______ 3. It turned out to be warmer today than I expected. I would have been warm in the sweater and uncomfortable in the tight flannel shirt. Wearing the sweatshirt was a good decision.

_______ 4. I will wear the sweatshirt.

_______ 5. A sweater, a flannel shirt, a sweatshirt.

_______ 6. What should I wear to school?

_______ 7. The sweatshirt would be the best choice.

A. Define the issue.
B. Make a self-inventory.
C. List all possible alternatives.
D. Forecast the outcome of each alternative.
E. Choose the best alternative.
F. Develop a plan of action.
G. Evaluate the results.

Choose one of the steps of the decision-making process. Explain what might happen if you fail to take that step when making an important decision.

____

____

____

____

When is it most helpful to use the decision-making process? Explain.

____

____

____

____

Describe situations when it would not be worthwhile to use the decision-making process.

____

____

____

____

Give an example of how the decision-making process could be used at work.

____

____

____

Trade-Offs

Activity C
Chapter 8

Name ______________________________
Date ________________ **Period** __________

For every decision you make, there are trade-offs. Read the decisions listed below and describe one trade-off for each decision.

1. To lose 10 pounds in a month

____

____

2. To get a driver's license within two weeks

____

____

3. To go to Europe on spring break

____

____

4. To get a job immediately after graduating from high school

____

____

5. To make the honor roll next grading period

____

____

6. To play a video game after school

____

____

7. To save $4,000 in one year for a car

____

____

8. To learn to dance in four weeks

____

____

9. To buy a new outfit this month

____

____

10. To complete all homework during study periods at school

____

____

Preparing for Career Decisions

Activity D
Chapter 8

Name ______________________________
Date ________________ **Period** __________

Planning ahead is the key to making a satisfying career decision. By starting to think about a career now, you will be better prepared to make decisions in the future. Start planning for your career by answering the following questions.

1. What courses and programs will you take in high school? ______________________________

2. How much effort will you put into your studies? ______________________________

3. What skills will you develop? ______________________________

4. What education and training beyond high school do you want to pursue? ______________________________

5. What careers will you explore? ______________________________

Making Decisions at Work

Activity E Name ____________________

Chapter 8 Date ______________ Period __________

Some decisions at work are easy to make, but other decisions require more careful thought. The more you practice making those difficult decisions, the easier they will become. Read the case studies that follow and answer the questions to complete the decision-making process.

Case Study I

Jeannie has just begun a new job as an air conditioning and heating technician's assistant. Jeannie's job is to get the tools ready for her boss. She is also expected to clean up the work area at the end of the day. During the day, other workers ask Jeannie to get materials for them. She helps stock supplies at the job site. Sometimes Jeannie does errands for the senior technicians on the job.

Jeannie's work area is often left dirty at the end of the day. Sometimes she keeps her boss from leaving work on time. She is often late in putting away the equipment. Lately, her supervisor has been reprimanding her quite often. Jeannie may not get a raise at the next salary review if her work has not improved.

1. What decision does Jeannie have to make? ____________________

2. What are her alternatives? ____________________

3. What are the trade-offs for each alternative? ____________________

4. What is the probable outcome of each alternative? ____________________

5. What decision would you make if you were in Jeannie's place? ____________________

6. Why would you make this decision? ____________________

(Continued)

Name ______________________________

Case Study II

Henry is a senior in a cooperative education program. He has been working for four weeks as a word processor in an office. Henry is one of six cooperative education students employed by the firm. Henry has much better office skills than the other students.

It is time for Ms. Jacobs, Henry's boss, to evaluate him and determine his continued employment. She has reviewed his file and has found that Henry does far more work than any of the other students. However, she has also noted that Henry is nearly 15 minutes late every day.

When talking to Henry, Ms. Jacobs once asked Henry why he was late every day. Henry replied, "I do more work than any other part-time worker here. I don't think it should matter if I come in late. I get the same pay and do more work. It's not fair that I work as long as the others."

Ms. Jacobs sees Henry's lateness as a serious problem. She is afraid the other students will begin to come in late if Henry continues to do so. On the other hand, she sees Henry's skills as an asset to the company.

1. What decision does Henry's boss have to make? ______________________________

2. What are her alternatives? ______________________________

3. What are the trade-offs for each alternative? ______________________________

4. What is the probable outcome of each alternative? ______________________________

5. What decision would you make if you were Henry's boss? ______________________________

6. Why would you make this decision? ______________________________

Chapter 9
Options for Education and Training

Reinforcing Vocabulary

Activity A | **Name** ____________________
Chapter 9 | **Date** ____________ **Period** ________

Match the following terms with their correct definitions.

_______ 1. Training offered by the U.S. Government for members of the Navy, Army, Air Force, Marines, or Coast Guard.
_______ 2. Training program that prepares employees to do a specialized job within their company.
_______ 3. Skills, such as reading, writing, and math, which are required for any career.
_______ 4. Training that involves learning a trade by working under the direction and guidance of a skilled worker.
_______ 5. Degree usually received after completing two years of education beyond high school.
_______ 6. Programs in the areas of health, business, agriculture, skilled trades, and marketing that may be offered to students who are still in high school.
_______ 7. Degree usually received after completing a four-year program beyond high school.
_______ 8. An arrangement between schools and places of employment that allows students to receive on-the-job training.
_______ 9. Institutions of higher learning that offer an associate degree.
_______ 10. Institutions of higher learning that offer bachelor's, master's, and doctorate degrees.
_______ 11. A student seeking skills for a career, who works in a temporary position with an emphasis on on-the-job training rather than employment.

A. apprenticeship
B. associate degree
C. bachelor's degree
D. basic skills
E. career/technical training
F. colleges and universities
G. community and junior college
H. company training program
I. cooperative education
J. intern
K. military training

Basic Skills for the Workplace

Activity B
Chapter 9

Name ____________________
Date ____________ **Period** ________

Basic reading, writing, and math skills are necessary in all jobs. To be a successful worker, you will need these skills as well as occupational skills. Complete the charts below by identifying two occupations that interest you. List the tasks that you think people do in those occupations and the basic skills needed for those tasks. Then decide whether you have the skills needed to perform those tasks.

Occupation 1: ____________________

Tasks	Basic Skills Needed
1. ____________	____________
____________	____________
2. ____________	____________
____________	____________
3. ____________	____________
____________	____________

Do you have the skills needed to perform the tasks listed above? If not, what can you do now to develop the skills? ____________________

Occupation 2: ____________________

Tasks	Basic Skills Needed
1. ____________	____________
____________	____________
2. ____________	____________
____________	____________
3. ____________	____________
____________	____________

Do you have the skills needed to perform the tasks listed above? If not, what can you do now to develop the skills? ____________________

Plans for Career Training

Activity C
Chapter 9

Name ______________________________
Date ____________________ **Period** ____________

Many different forms of career training are available, but the best training for you depends on your personal career goals. Name a career area that interests you. Then, for each type of training program listed below, identify the different employment opportunities within your career area that you would be qualified to pursue.

Student's career interest: ______________________________

Apprenticeships:

____
____
____

Four-year colleges and universities:

____
____
____

Two-year community and junior colleges:

____
____
____

Cooperative education:

____
____
____

Internships:

____
____
____

Military training:

____
____
____

Career/technical programs:

____
____
____

Figuring Education and Training Costs

Activity D
Chapter 9

Name ______________________
Date ______________ **Period** __________

Use this form to estimate the cost of higher education. Choose a program of study that interests you and is offered at a nearby school. Contact the school to learn about the program and related school costs. Then answer the following questions.

1. What program interests you? ______________________
2. At which nearby school would you take this program? ______________________
3. What is the address of the school? ______________________
4. Would you live at home, on school property, or some other location? ______________________
5. What would room and board cost for the first year? ______________________
6. Would you travel to school via public transportation? (If no, how would you get to school?) ______________________
7. What travel costs do you estimate for the first year? (If travel involves the purchase or lease of an automobile, include purchase/lease costs, insurance, taxes, parking fees, and all other associated costs.) ______________________
8. How much would you budget for clothing for one year? ______________________
9. How much would you budget for health care for one year? ______________________
10. How much would you budget for recreational activities for one year? ______________________
11. What are the **estimated related costs** (total of Questions 5–10)? ______________________
12. What is the cost of one-year's tuition? ______________________
13. Are there any special program fees? ______________________
14. Are there any required student fees? ______________________
15. What will schoolbooks and school supplies cost for the first year? ______________________
16. What is the **estimated school cost** (total of Questions 12–15)? ______________________
17. What is the **estimated first-year cost** for advanced education (total of Questions 11 and 16)? ______________________
18. Of the many options open to you, how would you pay for the first year of advanced education? ______________________

Chapter 10
Making a Career Plan

Reinforcing Vocabulary

Activity A
Chapter 10

Name ____________________
Date ______________ **Period** __________

Fill in the blanks with the correct chapter terms. Then give examples where requested.

1. ______________ resources are qualities or abilities that people have within themselves that can help them achieve goals. Two examples are the following: ______________
____
____

2. ______________ resources are material resources that can help people achieve goals. Two examples are the following: ______________
____

3. ______________ are aims or targets a person tries to reach or achieve.
A ______________ ______________ is an aim or target that will take more than six months to accomplish. Two examples are the following: ______________
____
____

4. A ______________ ______________ is a target that can be accomplished within a few days, weeks, or months. Two examples are the following: ______________
____
____

5. A ______________ ______________ is something you want to achieve for yourself. Two examples are the following: ______________
____

6. A ______________ ______________ is a target you want to reach in your career. Two examples might be the following: ______________
____

7. A ______________ ______________ is a list of steps you need to take to reach your career goal. It should include the following three items: ______________
A. ______________
B. ______________
C. ______________

Job Likes and Dislikes

Activity B **Name** ______________________________
Chapter 10 **Date** ________________ **Period** __________

Knowing your strong likes and dislikes will help you make a good career choice. Use the following checklist to see what kinds of jobs you would like most. If you would like the work situation described, place a check in the *likes* column. If you would not like the work described, place a check in the *dislikes* column.

Likes	Dislikes	
______	______	1. Work with many people
______	______	2. Talk to people at work
______	______	3. Work alone
______	______	4. Work inside
______	______	5. Work outside
______	______	6. Repair or make things
______	______	7. Work at one place
______	______	8. Travel to many worksites
______	______	9. Work regular hours
______	______	10. Work varied hours
______	______	11. Work days
______	______	12. Work nights
______	______	13. Work while standing or walking
______	______	14. Work while sitting
______	______	15. Work in a quiet place
______	______	16. Handle physical work
______	______	17. Handle mental work
______	______	18. Work with heavy machinery
______	______	19. Work with office equipment
______	______	20. Work in areas that may be dirty
______	______	21. Work in areas that are always clean
______	______	22. Work close to home
______	______	23. Work in a secure job
______	______	24. Work in a job that requires personal risks or challenges
______	______	25. Work in a job that will provide recognition by many people
______	______	26. Work for a large company
______	______	27. Work for a small company
______	______	28. Work in a job that requires special training
______	______	29. Work in a job that requires no special training
______	______	30. Work in a job free of hazards
______	______	31. Work in a job that may sometimes be dangerous
______	______	32. Work in a job that involves children
______	______	33. Work in a job that helps people
______	______	34. Work in a job that teaches/instructs people
______	______	35. Work in a job that informs people
______	______	36. Work in a job that sells goods
______	______	37. Work in a large city
______	______	38. Work in a small city or town
______	______	39. Work in a rural setting

(Continued)

Name ______________________________

Based on the checklist on the previous page, describe the type of job you want.______________________

Career Interests and Abilities Inventory

Activity C **Name** ____________________
Chapter 10 **Date** ____________ **Period** ________

Your interests and abilities can lead you to a career that will be fun and exciting for you. List three of your interests or abilities that relate to each area below. Then list one job you might like based on each interest or ability.

My Interests and Abilities	Related Jobs I Might Like
Hobbies	
1. ____________	1. ____________
2. ____________	2. ____________
3. ____________	3. ____________
Leisure activities	
1. ____________	1. ____________
2. ____________	2. ____________
3. ____________	3. ____________
Favorite school subjects	
1. ____________	1. ____________
2. ____________	2. ____________
3. ____________	3. ____________
Part-time or volunteer work	
1. ____________	1. ____________
2. ____________	2. ____________
3. ____________	3. ____________
Special abilities	
1. ____________	1. ____________
2. ____________	2. ____________
3. ____________	3. ____________

Setting and Reaching Goals

Activity D
Chapter 10

Name ____________________
Date ____________ **Period** ________

You make things happen by setting goals and making plans for reaching them. Think about your goals by completing this activity. Your responses will not be graded.

1. List five goals you would like to accomplish within the next few months.
   A. ____________________
   B. ____________________
   C. ____________________
   D. ____________________
   E. ____________________
2. List five goals you would like to accomplish within the next five to ten years.
   A. ____________________
   B. ____________________
   C. ____________________
   D. ____________________
   E. ____________________

(Continued)

Name ______________________________

3. Select the one goal from each list that is most important to you. Write these two goals in the space provided. Use checks to show whether each goal is personal or professional and short-term or long-term.

Most Important Goals	Professional Goal	Short-Term Goal	Long-Term Goal	Personal Goal
A.				
B.				

4. Select the one goal that is most important to you and write it as a statement. Indicate the date you want to reach this goal.

____

____

____

____

5. Decide how you will reach your goal and write a detailed plan.

____

____

____

____

____

____

____

____

____

____

____

____

____

____

____

____

____

____

____

Chapter 11
Job Search Skills

Reinforcing Vocabulary

Activity A Name ______________________________
Chapter 11 Date ________________ Period __________

Write each of the following terms from the chapter in the blank in front of its definition.

closed ad
electronic bulletin boards
job application form
networking
open ad
portfolio
private employment agency
public employment service
references
résumé
want ads

______________________ 1. A business that helps people find jobs for a fee.

______________________ 2. A government-supported group that helps people find jobs for free.

______________________ 3. These allow you to post and read messages on the computer, acting as a media for the exchange of information among large groups of people, combining the features of electronic mail with private computer conferencing.

______________________ 4. A formal written summary of a person's education, work experience, and other qualifications for a job.

______________________ 5. People who can speak about a person's character and skills.

______________________ 6. A selection of materials that you can use to document your accomplishments over a period of time.

______________________ 7. A form completed by a job applicant to provide an employer with information about the applicant's background.

______________________ 8. A source of information about available jobs, found in the classified section of the newspaper.

______________________ 9. A classified ad providing specific information about a job.

______________________ 10. A classified ad giving general information about a job.

______________________ 11. Checking with family, friends, and other people you know to find out about job openings.

Want Ad Abbreviations

Activity B
Chapter 11

Name ______________________________
Date ____________________ **Period** __________

Many want ads use abbreviations to save space. Study the abbreviations listed in Figure 11-2 of the text. Then read each ad below and write out the entire ad without using abbreviations. Use a dictionary to look up any unfamiliar abbreviations.

1. Temp., p/t help wanted. No exp. nec., co. will train. Some eve. hrs., good sal., light wk. Call 555-1212.

____
____
____
____
____

2. F/T ofc. wk., oppty. to grow into mgr. position. Some bkkg. exp. nec., keyboard 50 wpm. Call Ms. Jones between 9 a.m. and 3 p.m. at 555-6677.

____
____
____
____
____

3. Immed. opening for asst. mgr. Ex. benefits, sal. neg. Refs. & 5 yrs. exp. req. (EOE) Joe's Fast Foods, call Mr. Banks 555-6273.

____
____
____
____
____

Using Want Ads

Activity C
Chapter 11

Name ____________________
Date ____________ **Period** ________

Find the classified section in your local newspaper and locate the want ads. Find an ad that matches your interests and level of education and mount it in the space below. Use the ad to answer the questions that follow.

1. What is the title of the advertised job? ____________________
2. What salary is listed or expected for this job? ____________________
3. What education is required for this job? ____________________
4. What job requirements are listed? ____________________
5. What strengths do you possess for this job? ____________________
6. Whom should you contact for further information concerning this job? ____________________
7. What further training might you need for this job? ____________________
8. How can you get more information about the company before you make contact with them? ____________________
9. What questions should you be prepared to answer when you make contact with the company? ____________________
10. What additional information about this job would you request? ____________________

Résumé Worksheet

Activity D
Chapter 11

Name ______________________
Date ______________ **Period** __________

Develop your own résumé by filling in the information requested. Follow the guidelines given in the text. You may include optional information if you wish. Ask a friend or relative to read over your résumé and give you suggestions. Then type or neatly print your final résumé on your own paper.

Name: ______________________

Address: ______________________

Telephone number: ______________________

Employment:

____

____

____

____

____

____

Education:

____

____

____

____

____

____

Activities and Honors:

____

____

____

Hobbies:

____

____

References:

____

____

____

____

____

Applying for Employment

Activity E
Chapter 11

Name ______________________
Date ____________ **Period** ________

Complete this application for employment. Print clearly and fill in all the requested information. Apply for an employment opportunity in your interest area.

APPLICATION FOR EMPLOYMENT

PERSONAL INFORMATION

Name ____
Last First Middle

Present Address ______________________________________
Street City State Zip

Telephone ____
Area

JOB INTEREST

Position for which you are applying: ______________________

Salary desired: ______________ Date you can start: ______________

Have you ever been employed by this company before? ______________

If yes, where? ______________ When? ______________

EDUCATION AND TRAINING

Name and Address of School	Number of Years Completed	Major Studies
Grade School		
High School		
Trade or Business School		
College		

EMPLOYMENT RECORD

Name and Address of Employers Beginning with Your Most Recent Employer	Type of Work	Dates Employed	Reason for Leaving

(Continued)

Name ______________________________

If you have served in the U.S. Armed Forces, indicate:

Branch ______________________________ Special Training ______________________________

Rank Attained ______________________________ Years in Service ______________________________

Honors or Awards ______________________________ Date of Separation ______________________________

REFERENCES (List the names of three people not related to you whom you have known at least one year.)

Name	Address	Phone Number	Occupation	Years Known

ADDITIONAL DATA

Have you ever been convicted of a crime (other than traffic, game law, or other minor violations)? ________

If yes, explain the offense and circumstances regarding the conviction: ______________________________

Is your age under 18? ______________________________

Are you a U.S. Citizen? ______________________________

If no, do you have an alien registration card or valid U.S. work permit? ______________________________

Non-English languages you read ______________ speak ______________ write ______________

Special skills, knowledge, and abilities that qualify you for the position you are seeking: ______________

____

____

PHYSICAL STATUS

Are you presently or have you during the last six months been under a physician's care or in a hospital?

____

Have you ever been compensated for, or do you currently have outstanding, a job-related claim? ________

If yes to any of the above, explain: ______________________________

____

Thank you for completing this application form and for your interest in employment with us. We would like to assure you that your opportunity for employment with this company will be based only on your merit without regard to your race, religion, sex, age, national origin, or disability.

PLEASE READ CAREFULLY
APPLICANT'S CERTIFICATION AND AGREEMENT

I certify that the facts contained in this application are true and complete to the best of my knowledge. I understand that, if employed, falsified statements on this application shall be grounds for dismissal.

I authorize investigation of all statements contained in this application. I authorize the references listed above to give you any and all information concerning my previous employment and any pertinent information they may have, personal or otherwise. I release all parties from all liability for any damage that may result from furnishing this information to you.

Date __________ Signature of applicant ______________________________

Chapter 12
Interviewing Skills

Reinforcing Vocabulary

Activity A **Name** ______________________
Chapter 12 **Date** ______________ **Period** __________

Match the following terms with their correct definitions.

________	1. A talk between an employer and a job applicant.	A. follow-up letter
________	2. The company representative who talks with job applicants.	B. job description
________	3. Telephone conversation between a company representative and a job applicant.	C. interview
________	4. Face-to-face meeting between an employer and a job applicant.	D. interviewee
________	5. An explanation of tasks to be performed by an employee in a specific position.	E. interviewer
________	6. A brief letter written in business form to thank the interviewer for the interview.	F. personal interview
________	7. A job applicant who receives an interview.	G. telephone interview

Write a one- or two-paragraph story about someone who is looking for a job. Correctly use all the above vocabulary terms in your story.

Company Research

Activity B **Name** ______________________________
Chapter 12 **Date** ________________ **Period** __________

Select a company at which you would like to work and a job that you would like to have. Research the company and the job. Then provide the information requested below.

1. At what company would you like to work? ______________________________

____

2. Why would you like to work there? ______________________________

____

____

3. What job would you like to have? ______________________________
4. Why do you think you would like this job? ______________________________

____

____

5. What skills are needed for this job? ______________________________

____

6. List any needed skills you are lacking and describe how you could acquire them. ______________________________

____

____

7. What products does the company produce, or what services does it offer? ______________________________
8. Have you ever used these products or services? If so, explain why you were or were not satisfied. ____

____

9. How many people are employed by the company? ______________________________
10. Does the company have plans for future growth or expansion? ______________________________
11. What opportunities for advancement would be available to you? ______________________________

____

12. List five questions you would ask if you were being interviewed for a job with this company. __________

A. ______________________________

____

B. ______________________________

____

C. ______________________________

____

D. ______________________________

____

E. ______________________________

____

Interview Questions

Activity C
Chapter 12

Name ______________________
Date ____________ **Period** ________

Interviewers often ask job applicants the following questions. Answer each of the questions as though you were on a job interview. Discuss your answers in class.

1. Why do you want to work here? ______________________

2. Tell me about yourself. ______________________

3. What are your favorite subjects in school? ______________________

4. What are your least favorite subjects in school? ______________________

5. What do you like to do in your free time? ______________________

6. Tell me about some of your other jobs. ______________________

7. Why did you leave your last job? ______________________

8. What are your major strengths? ______________________

9. What are your weaknesses? ______________________

10. What do you want to do five years from now? ______________________

Interview Practices

Activity D **Name** ____________________
Chapter 12 **Date** ____________ **Period** ________

Listed below are a variety of interview situations. Read each situation and decide whether the interview practice being described is a good practice or a poor one. In the blank space preceding each statement, either write *G* for good or *P* for poor. For those you mark *P*, use the space provided to explain what the interviewee should have done differently.

______ 1. As Glenn walked into the interviewer's office, he said, "I sure am tired. I gotta sit down and have a cigarette. Ya gotta light?"

______ 2. William arrived for his interview 15 minutes early. After giving his name to the receptionist, he quietly waited until he was called for his interview.

______ 3. Because Jackie was babysitting her two-year-old brother, she brought him along to her interview.

______ 4. After a fun day at the beach, Blake hurried to his interview at the drugstore wearing brightly colored shorts and no shirt.

______ 5. When Joan interviewed at Hamburger Heaven, she said, "Ya know, I've eaten your hamburgers and they're really gross."

______ 6. When Katie interviewed for the receptionist's job, she said, "I don't have experience answering business phones, but I love talking with people and I'm willing to learn."

______ 7. Raymond was nervous at his first job interview. He looked at the wall instead of the interviewer and gave simple yes and no answers to the questions he was asked.

______ 8. Brian said to the interviewer, "I would do a good job as a groundskeeper for your company. For three years, I have had my own outdoor maintenance service, and all my customers have been satisfied."

(Continued)

Name ______________________________

_________ 9. The interviewer told Sally to make herself comfortable, so she sprawled out on the couch and began chewing bubble gum.

____

____

_________ 10. Tom told the interviewer at A to Z Dry Cleaners that he and his family have always gotten excellent service there.

____

____

_________ 11. Melanie said to the interviewer, "I want to be a candy striper because I like helping people and would like to become a nurse."

____

____

_________ 12. Carla came to her interview for the typing position wearing a neatly pressed skirt and blouse.

____

____

_________ 13. James told the interviewer, "I'm sorry I'm late, but I overslept."

____

____

_________ 14. Marta said to the interviewer, "I'll take anything. I don't care what I do."

____

____

_________ 15. Amy said to the interviewer, "What hours would I work? I sleep until noon, so I can't get to work until 1 p.m."

____

____

Follow-Up in Writing

Activity E
Chapter 12

Name ______________________________
Date ____________________ **Period** ____________

Bob Johnson just completed an interview for a sales position with Joseph Sebastian, human resources manager for Watson's Department Store. Watson's is located at 735 S. River Road in Bently, Nebraska 00923. Bob lives nearby at 832 W. Roseville Drive in Bently.

Bob had heard he should send a follow-up letter after an interview, so he wrote the letter below. Bob had the right idea, but his letter needs a little work. Read his letter and answer the questions that follow.

Dear Joe,

Thanks for the interview. You seem like a nice guy, and the job sounded kinda fun. I wouldn't mind working for you. Let me know if I get the job.

Sincerely,

Bob Johnson

What suggestions would you give Bob for improving his letter?

____

____

____

Write a follow-up letter for Bob that might give Mr. Sebastian a better impression. (Use another sheet of paper if you need more space.)

____

____

____

____

____

____

____

____

____

____

____

____

____

____

____

____

Chapter 13
Good Employee Skills

Reinforcing Vocabulary

Activity A
Chapter 13

Name ______________________________
Date ________________ **Period** __________

Read each of the definitions below and decide which chapter term is being defined. Write the correct terms in the crossword puzzle.

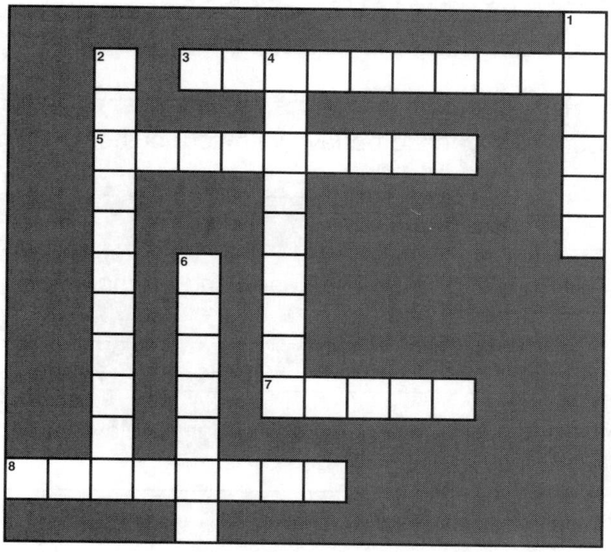

Across

3. Being reliable.
5. A ______ is a severe expression of disapproval.
7. A work ______ is a standard of conduct and values for job performance.
8. A person who is ______ comes to work on time.

Down

1. A more experienced person who provides his or her expertise in order to help less-experienced workers advance in their careers, enhance their education, and build networks.
2. The end of employment or the loss of a job is called ______.
4. A right that is given to an employee as a benefit or favor is a ______.
6. A ______ is a loss or hardship for breaking company rules and policies.

If You Were an Employer

Activity B
Chapter 13

Name ____________________
Date ____________ **Period** ________

Imagine you are the owner of a small business. Answer the following questions about the expectations you would have for your employees.

1. What type of business would you own? ____________________
2. What traits would you want your employees to have? ____________________
3. How would you expect your employees to behave with one another? ____________________
4. How would you expect your employees to behave with you? ____________________
5. How would you expect your employees to behave with your customers and business contacts? ____________________
6. What kind of employees would you reward with raises and promotions? ____________________
7. What company rules and policies would you have for your employees? ____________________
8. What kinds of penalties would you have for employees who broke your rules and policies? ____________________
9. Under what circumstances would you fire an employee? ____________________
10. What time would you expect your employees to begin work each day? ____________________
11. What kinds of privileges would you extend to your employees? ____________________
12. Do you think your employees would enjoy working for you? Explain your answer. ____________________

Chapter 14
Being a Team Player

Reinforcing Vocabulary

Activity A **Name** ____________________
Chapter 14 **Date** ____________ **Period** ________

Complete the following definitions by writing the missing term in the preceding blanks.

argumentative	constructive criticism	ridicule
brainstorming	gossip	rumor
compromise	grapevine	sarcasm
conflict	harassment	teamwork

______________ 1. The process of _____ involves listing everyone's ideas, no matter how ridiculous the ideas may seem, and then discussing and evaluating them.

______________ 2. The use of cutting remarks is _____.

______________ 3. When you _____, you tell personal information about another person.

______________ 4. Two or more people working toward a common goal is known as _____.

______________ 5. To _____ a person is to make fun of him or her.

______________ 6. A person who disagrees with just about everything can be described as _____.

______________ 7. Offering judgmental remarks about a person or his or her work is _____.

______________ 8. A bit of information that passes from one person to another without proof of accuracy is a _____.

______________ 9. An informal and unofficial flow of information is called a _____.

______________ 10. A _____ is a hostile situation resulting from opposing views.

______________ 11. Doing or saying things that make people feel different or uncomfortable is _____.

______________ 12. Giving something up to resolve a conflict is _____.

Tips for Getting Along

Activity B **Name** ______________________________
Chapter 14 **Date** ____________________ **Period** __________

Interview three people who each work in a different occupation. Ask each person to give five important tips for getting along with coworkers. List their responses in the space provided.

Occupation of First Person: ______________________________

First Person's Tips:

1. ______________________________
2. ______________________________
3. ______________________________
4. ______________________________
5. ______________________________

Occupation of Second Person: ______________________________

Second Person's Tips:

1. ______________________________
2. ______________________________
3. ______________________________
4. ______________________________
5. ______________________________

Occupation of Third Person: ______________________________

Third Person's Tips:

1. ______________________________
2. ______________________________
3. ______________________________
4. ______________________________
5. ______________________________

Why might some of the tips from the three people be similar? ______________________________

____

Why might some of the tips you were given be different? ______________________________

____

Do you agree with the tips listed above? Explain. ______________________________

____

____

Do you disagree with any of the tips listed? Explain. ______________________________

____

____

____

Studying Work Attitudes

Activity C **Name** ______________________

Chapter 14 **Date** ______________ **Period** ________

Carefully read each situation described below and respond to each request.

1. Imagine it is your first day on a new job. Describe what you would do to make a good impression on your coworkers and supervisors. Keep your answer in mind as you complete this activity.

____

____

____

____

____

____

2. Now consider David, a stock clerk in a large supermarket. David does only what he is told to do, no more and no less. Does David have a good attitude toward work? Explain.

____

____

____

3. One day, one of David's coworkers knocked over a product display. Boxes were scattered all over the floor. At the time, David was working nearby. If you were David, what should you have done in this situation?

____

____

____

4. David ignored the scattered boxes and left his workstation to tell others what had happened. David made a big joke at his coworker's expense. If you were David's supervisor, what would you say to David?

____

____

____

5. If you were the worker who knocked over the display, what would you have said to David?

____

____

____

6. Later the same day, David was stocking shelves. The product he was stocking belonged in another part of the store. A coworker trying to help David told him he was making a mistake. However, David insisted he was right and started an argument. Was it proper for David to argue with his coworker?

____

(Continued)

Name ______________________________

7. What do you think David should have done?

8. Before David went home that night, he overheard part of a conversation between two coworkers and their supervisor. The next morning, David told everyone what he had heard. The entire supermarket was soon exchanging comments on the news involving the coworkers. Was David correct in discussing what he had overheard? Explain.

9. When David's supervisor found out what had happened, she called David into her office for a conference. What do you think was said to David?

10. If you were one of David's coworkers, what advice would you give to David?

11. If you were David's supervisor, what would you do to help David become a better employee? Explain.

Good Work Habits in Action

Activity D
Chapter 14

Name ______________________________
Date ________________ **Period** __________

In your own words, explain how having the work habits listed below can help you get along with your coworkers. Give a specific example of how you could put each work habit into action.

Work Habits	Effect on Coworkers	Work Habits in Action
1. Being open to new ideas		
2. Respecting coworkers		
3. Seeing coworkers' positive qualities		
4. Showing trust		
5. Admitting errors		
6. Accepting constructive criticism positively		

(Continued)

Name ____________________

Work Habits	Effect on Coworkers	Work Habits in Action
7. Keeping a positive attitude		
8. Having a good sense of humor		
9. Avoiding the poor use of humor		
10. Avoiding arguments		
11. Avoiding rumors		
12. Avoiding harassment		
13. Avoiding comparisons		

Chapter 15
Keeping Safety First

Reinforcing Vocabulary

Activity A Name ______________________
Chapter 15 Date ____________ Period ________

Match the following terms with their correct definitions.

_______ 1. Insurance against work-related accidents.
_______ 2. A liquid that can easily ignite and burn rapidly.
_______ 3. Oxygen, fuel, and heat: the three items that must be present for a fire to take place.
_______ 4. Describes a plug that has an electrical connection with the earth to prevent shock.
_______ 5. A national act that calls for safe and healthy working conditions; also the title of a government agency.
_______ 6. To empty or vacate a place in an organized manner for protection.
_______ 7. Immediate, temporary treatment given in the event of an accident or sudden illness.
_______ 8. A temporary or permanent physical or mental condition that prevents an employee from working.
_______ 9. Another term for being fired.
_______ 10. An act that protects the educational opportunities of youth and prohibits their employment in jobs that could endanger their health and safety.

A. disability
B. dismissal
C. evacuate
D. fire triangle
E. first aid
F. flammable liquid
G. FLSA
H. grounded
I. OSHA
J. workers' compensation

Preventing Accidents

Activity B
Chapter 15

Name ____________________
Date ____________ **Period** ________

Select six of the occupations listed below and write them in the chart. For each occupation selected, describe an accident that could occur. Then list what could be done to prevent the accident.

Chef
Salesclerk
Secretary
Nurse's aide
Gas station attendant
Police officer
Firefighter
Plumber
Electrician
Florist
Mason
Flight attendant
Pilot
Truck driver
Farmer
Bookkeeper
Painter
Baggage handler

Occupation	Possible Accident	Preventive Measure
1.		
2.		
3.		
4.		
5.		
6.		

Understanding Safety Practices

Activity C Name ______________________
Chapter 15 Date ____________ Period ________

Answer the following questions about safety on the job using the information provided in the chapter.

1. What should you do if you are not sure how to perform any part of your job? ______________________

2. Why might someone who is showing off be a hazard in the workplace? ______________________

3. How can open desk or file drawers be a hazard in a workplace? ______________________

4. Why shouldn't electrical machines or connections be touched with wet hands? ______________________

5. Why should workers avoid leaning too far back in their chairs? ______________________

6. Why should worn electrical cords or plugs be replaced? ______________________

7. Why should electrical connections not be unplugged by pulling the cord? ______________________

8. Why should electrical circuits not be overloaded with too many machines or appliances? ______________________

9. When working with machinery, why should clothes fit snugly? ______________________

10. Explain what type of shoes should be worn on industrial or construction work sites. ______________________

11. What six things should a smart worker know about lifting properly? ______________________

12. Why should safety goggles be worn when using electrical tools and equipment? ______________________

13. How should an object be lifted from the floor? ______________________

(Continued)

Name ______________________________

14. What types of accidents can occur in cluttered and messy work areas? ____________________

15. What safety devices should be used when mopping a floor? ____________________

16. Why should metal ladders not be used near electrical equipment or high-voltage wires? ____________________

17. How close to your work should you position a ladder? ____________________

18. What two hazards cause nearly half of all fires each year? ____________________

19. Why should oily rags and paper never be stored in open containers? ____________________

20. What is the correct way to use the telephone to report a fire? ____________________

21. What may happen if workers fail to wash their hands before eating or smoking? ____________________

22. Why should you stop working if you become ill on the job? ____________________

23. What should you do if you become injured on the job? ____________________

24. When giving first aid, why should you check to see that an injured person does not have anything in his or her mouth or throat? ____________________

25. Why was the Occupational Safety and Health Act passed? ____________________

26. Why must employers place the OSHA poster in the workplace? ____________________

27. What will workers' compensation cover if a worker is injured on the job? ____________________

Chapter 16
Handling Changes in Job Status

Reinforcing Vocabulary

Activity A — **Name** ______________________
Chapter 16 — **Date** ____________ **Period** ________

Match the following terms with their correct definitions.

_______ 1. Payment one-and-one-half or two times the regular wage that is given for hours worked beyond the normal 40-hour workweek.
_______ 2. A percentage of the dollar amount of sales made.
_______ 3. A set amount of money that is earned for a full year of work.
_______ 4. Being dismissed from a job for a reason beyond a worker's control, such as a cutback on production.
_______ 5. A letter written to inform an employer that an employee is quitting his or her job.
_______ 6. A set amount of money that is earned for every hour of work.
_______ 7. Being dismissed from a job due to poor performance or the inability to get along with others.

A. commission
B. fired
C. laid off
D. letter of resignation
E. overtime pay
F. salary
G. wages

Starting Full-Time Work

Activity B
Chapter 16

Name ______________________________
Date ____________________ **Period** ____________

Interview someone you know who has recently changed from part-time to full-time work. Record his or her answers to the questions that follow. Share what you learn with the class.

1. What caused you to change from part-time to full-time work? ______________________________

2. What do you like most about working full-time? ______________________________

3. What challenged you most when you first began working full-time? ______________________________

4. What changes surprised you when you became a full-time worker? ______________________________

5. How did your lifestyle change when you began working full-time? ______________________________

6. Based on what you learned, what advice would you give to someone preparing to change from part-time work to full-time work? ______________________________

Changing Jobs

Activity C
Chapter 16

Name ______________________________
Date ________________ **Period** __________

The statements listed below are possible advantages and disadvantages of changing jobs. Place an *A* before each advantage and a *D* before each disadvantage. Afterward, join a small group of your classmates and compare your answers with others in the group.

_______ 1. A new job is a chance for a new beginning.
_______ 2. A new job is a chance for growth and promotion.
_______ 3. You may have to move.
_______ 4. You may earn a higher salary.
_______ 5. You may have opportunities for retraining or advanced learning.
_______ 6. You may be labeled a job hopper.
_______ 7. You will have new experiences and face new challenges.
_______ 8. You may lose accumulated paid sick leave.
_______ 9. You may have to rebuild vacation time.
_______ 10. You may receive better fringe benefits.
_______ 11. You will be dealing with many unknowns.
_______ 12. You may be able to travel.
_______ 13. You will have the chance to build new friendships.
_______ 14. You may have to leave a job you like.
_______ 15. You may lose seniority rights.
_______ 16. You may not receive as many fringe benefits as in your present job.
_______ 17. You may spend less time commuting to work.
_______ 18. You may be the lowest-ranked person in the new job.

Leaving a Job

Activity D | **Name** ______________________
Chapter 16 | **Date** ______________ **Period** ________

Read the letter of resignation below, written by Joe Left, and answer the questions that follow. Then rewrite the letter.

> 49 Crooked Road
> Alsip, IL 60658
> November 15, 20xx
>
> Mr. Bruce Kovacs
> The Music Store
> 100 Harmony Road
> Alsip, IL 60658
>
> Dear Mr. Kovacs:
>
> I will be leaving at the end of this week. I have a much better job with Stereo-Recorder Company. You should have given me that raise I asked for yesterday. This wasn't such a great job, and I'm not sorry to leave.
>
> Sincerely,
>
> *Joe Left*

1. Did Joe give notice of his resignation far enough in advance? How much notice is recommended?
____
____
____

2. Is it acceptable for Joe to tell his employer that he has a better position? Explain. ______________
____
____
____

3. Should Joe have made the statement about the raise he didn't get? Explain. ______________
____
____

4. Explain what is wrong with Joe's last statement. ______________
____
____

On a separate sheet of paper, rewrite Joe's letter to convey his message in a more positive way.

Job Changes Through a Career

Activity E
Chapter 16

Name ______________________________
Date ____________________ **Period** ____________

Read the following case study about the various job changes experienced by one worker during his career. Answer the questions related to the case.

Case Study

After graduating from college, Allen got a job as a technical writer with a small company. Allen had been working for the company for about a year when it was purchased by a major corporation. When the new owners reorganized the business, Allen was laid off.

1. What positive action could Allen have taken after losing his job? ______________________________
____
____
____

Allen began a new job search and found a job as a laboratory assistant in a large company. Allen enjoyed his job, but he wanted to do more. He wanted to be promoted into the research and development group.

2. How could Allen prepare for the promotion he wanted?______________________________
____
____
____

Allen got his promotion and started working as part of a team to develop new product ideas. However, after four years, Allen is starting to think about changing jobs.

3. Why might Allen be thinking about changing jobs? ______________________________
____
____
____

4. What are some questions Allen should ask himself before making a decision to change jobs? ________
____
____
____

5. Once Allen decides for sure that he wants to change jobs, what should he do? ______________
____
____
____

Report on Changes

Activity F
Chapter 16

Name ______________________
Date ______________ **Period** __________

Read an article in a current magazine on one of the following topics:

- how to prepare for promotions
- what to do when you lose a job
- why people change jobs
- what other reasons cause changes in job status

Prepare a written report on the article and an oral report for the class. Be prepared to answer questions about the article.

Article title: ______________________

Author: ______________________

Source: ______________________

Report: ______________________

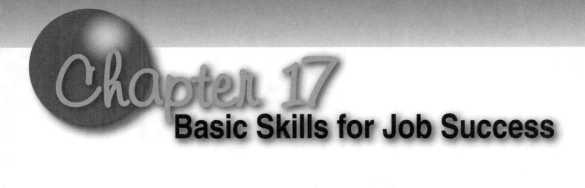

Chapter 17
Basic Skills for Job Success

Reinforcing Vocabulary

Activity A | **Name** ______________________
Chapter 17 | **Date** ____________ **Period** ________

Match the following terms with their correct definitions.

_____ 1. Metric unit of weight that is less than one ounce.
_____ 2. To read something and mark any errors found in it.
_____ 3. The group of words you know and use.
_____ 4. Metric unit that measures volume and is slightly more than a quart.
_____ 5. Word that describes a person who does not know how to read or write.
_____ 6. A decimal system of weights and measures that is used by many countries.
_____ 7. Metric unit that measures distance and is slightly longer than one yard.
_____ 8. Metric unit for measuring temperature that is a little more than two degrees Fahrenheit.

A. degrees Celsius
B. gram
C. illiterate
D. liter
E. meter
F. metric system
G. proofread
H. vocabulary

Strengthening Your Vocabulary

Activity B **Name** ______________________
Chapter 17 **Date** ______________ **Period** __________

Read the following article on "Nutrition Facts." List any words in the article that are unfamiliar to you in the spaces that follow. Find these words in a dictionary and write their definitions.

Nutrition Facts

Dietitians have determined that limiting your intake of fats can help reduce your risk of atherosclerosis. They recommend that no more than 30 percent of your daily caloric intake come from fats. The average adult woman needs about 2000 Calories each day. This means that no more than 600 of those Calories should come from fat. The average adult man needs about 2700 Calories each day. A man, therefore, should limit his daily fat intake to 810 Calories.

Nutrition labels on food can help you analyze how much fat you are eating. Nutrition labels list the number of grams of fat in a serving of food. Each gram of fat equals nine Calories. Therefore, using the recommendations above, the average woman should eat no more than 67 grams of fat per day. The average man should eat no more than 90 grams of fat.

What kinds of foods are high in fats? Whole milk dairy products, choice grade meats, and desserts are some of the biggest culprits. One cup of whole milk contains eight grams of fat. A three-ounce piece of chuck roast may contain 26 grams of fat. A piece of cheesecake has about 18 grams of fat.

Don't let these figures make you too apprehensive. You can always fill up on fruits and vegetables! Foods like apples, oranges, carrots, and peas contain only traces of fat, and they are full of vitamins, minerals, and fiber.

Words	Definitions
1. ______________	______________
2. ______________	______________
3. ______________	______________
4. ______________	______________
5. ______________	______________

Proofreading for Accuracy

Activity C **Name** ______________________________
Chapter 17 **Date** ________________ **Period** __________

Proofread the following sentences. Mark any grammar, spelling, or punctuation errors you find. Then rewrite the sentences correctly. The first sentence has been done for you.

Example: When the dog tracks mud into the house Mrs Carson gets angry.
<u>When the dog tracks mud into the house, Mrs. Carson gets angry.</u>

1. When a student does not do their homework, they are given a detention.

____

____

2. Running, swimming, and bicycles are good forms of exersize.

____

____

3. "Stop! she yelled.

____

____

4. A cat will clean itself by licking it's fir.

____

____

5. Clarence and Jim knows about the surprise there teacher has for the class.

____

____

6. The room was pink and and green.

____

____

7. He wont go no matter how many times you ask him.

____

____

8. The project was due Tuesday march 27.

____

____

9. Your going to the store after work, aren't you.

____

____

Math Practice

Activity D
Chapter 17

Name ______________________________
Date __________________ **Period** __________

Practice using your math skills by solving the following problems. Do not use a calculator.

1. 25
   73
   12
   +6

2. 39.5
   +6.2

3. 1/3 + 1/7 =

4. 943
   −21

5. 9.03
   −.72

6. 5/12 − 1/4 =

7. 886
   ×62

8. 7.2
   ×5.9

9. 1/3 × 1/2 =

10. 52)1144

11. .5)10.45

12. 3/8 ÷ 2 =

13. Write 0.66 as a percentage. ______________________________
14. Write 91% as a decimal. ______________________________
15. Suppose you, as a cashier, are given a five dollar bill for a $3.52 purchase. What coins and bills should you return to the customer? ______________________________
16. Suppose you, as a cashier, are given a $20 bill for a $16.71 purchase. What coins and bills should you return to the customer? ______________________________
17. Suppose you, as a cashier, are given a $20 bill and a $10 bill for a $22.43 purchase. What coins and bills should you return to the customer? ______________________________
18. Convert 6 inches to centimeters. ______________________________
19. Convert 52 kilograms to pounds. ______________________________
20. Convert 13 gallons to liters. ______________________________

Chapter 18
Time Management and Study Skills

Reinforcing Vocabulary

Activity A | **Name** ______________________
Chapter 18 | **Date** ____________ **Period** ________

Complete the following definitions by writing the missing term in the preceding blanks.

attitude	memory	tests
concentrate	priorities	time
IRS time	procrastination	time log
key	review	time management

______________ 1. To focus your effort and attention on something is to _____.

______________ 2. Poor use of _____ is a common cause of poor study habits.

______________ 3. Do not rely on your _____ to recall important things to do.

______________ 4. All the things you consider highly important are _____.

______________ 5. When taking notes, listen carefully and write down the _____ points.

______________ 6. Delaying decisions or activities is _____.

______________ 7. The purpose of _____ is to measure how much you know and don't know.

______________ 8. _____ _____ is short for Individual Responsibility for Saving Time. It involves taking steps to make the best use of your time.

______________ 9. After you study, take time to mentally _____ the material.

______________ 10. A written record of a person's use of time is a(n) _____ _____.

______________ 11. Planning and carefully using time is called _____ _____.

______________ 12. A positive _____ will help you begin your study assignment.

Time Log

Activity B
Chapter 18

Name ______________________________
Date _______________ **Period** __________

Learn how you spend your time by keeping a time log for one week. Fill in the blocks in the chart below to indicate the amount of time you spend each day with each activity. Indicate time in hours to the nearest quarter-hour (15 minutes = .25 hour; 30 minutes = .50 hour; 45 minutes = .75 hour). Remember that the total time spent for all your combined activities should equal 24 hours each day. At the end of the week, total your time for each activity.

	Sun	Mon	Tues	Wed	Thurs	Fri	Sat	Total Hours
Sleeping								
Eating								
Grooming								
Going to school								
Studying or doing homework								
Working at a job								
Doing household tasks								
Participating in extracurricular activities								
Watching TV or listening to music								
Phoning/messaging friends								
Visiting friends								
Reading and relaxing								
Doing other activities								
Total Number of Hours	24	24	24	24	24	24	24	168

Time Log Review

Activity C
Chapter 18

Name ________________________________
Date __________________ **Period** __________

Review the time log you completed in Activity B. Then answer the questions that follow as you refer to the time log.

1. What activity used the most time? ________________________________
2. How many hours did you spend doing chores?
   A. Average hours per day: ________________________________
   B. Total weekly hours: ________________________________
3. How many hours did you spend doing homework and studying?
   A. Average hours per day: ________________________________
   B. Total weekly hours: ________________________________
4. How many hours did you spend taking part in extracurricular activities?
   A. Average hours per day: ________________________________
   B. Total weekly hours: ________________________________
5. How many hours did you spend working?
   A. Average hours per day: ________________________________
   B. Total weekly hours: ________________________________
6. How many hours did you spend watching TV, listening to music, and surfing the Internet?
   A. Average hours per day: ________________________________
   B. Total weekly hours: ________________________________
7. How many hours did you spend reading and relaxing?
   A. Average hours per day: ________________________________
   B. Total weekly hours: ________________________________
8. How many hours did you spend visiting friends?
   A. Average hours per day: ________________________________
   B. Total weekly hours: ________________________________
9. How many hours do you usually sleep per day? ________________________________
10. About how much time do you spend eating each day? ________________________________
11. About how much time do you spend grooming each day? ________________________________
12. About how many hours per day do you spend talking on the phone? ________________________________
13. About how much total weekly time do you spend doing other activities? ________________________________
14. Are you spending your time on your most important priorities? ________________________________
15. When do you usually do your homework and study? Is this the best time of day for you to study?

    ____

(Continued)

Name ________________________________

16. Do you usually spend more time doing homework and studying or working? ____________________
17. Do you spend enough time studying? ____
18. Do you spend enough time relaxing? ____
19. Do you spend enough time doing chores? ____
20. Which activities are taking up too much of your time? Can you reduce the time spent on these activities?

    ____

    ____

    ____

21. Are you usually able to complete important tasks on time? ___________________________
22. Are you a good time manager now? ____
23. What daily habits would you like to change to improve the use of your time? ______________

    ____

24. What new habits can you develop to give yourself more free time? _____________________

    ____

25. How could you use the free time gained? ____

    ____

26. What steps can you take to make your study time more effective? _____________________

    ____

    ____

    ____

IRS Time

Activity D
Chapter 18

Name ______________________
Date ______________ **Period** __________

Place yourself on IRS Time by filling in the following "To Do" list with all the tasks you want to accomplish within the next week. Check the A column for tasks that you absolutely must do, the B column for tasks that you should do next, and the C column for tasks you will do if there is time. Follow your list for two days, checking off tasks as you complete them. Then answer the questions at the bottom of the page.

Priority					
A	**B**	**C**		**To Do**	**Completed**
____	____	____	1.	______________________	________
____	____	____	2.	______________________	________
____	____	____	3.	______________________	________
____	____	____	4.	______________________	________
____	____	____	5.	______________________	________
____	____	____	6.	______________________	________
____	____	____	7.	______________________	________
____	____	____	8.	______________________	________
____	____	____	9.	______________________	________
____	____	____	10.	______________________	________
____	____	____	11.	______________________	________
____	____	____	12.	______________________	________
____	____	____	13.	______________________	________
____	____	____	14.	______________________	________
____	____	____	15.	______________________	________
____	____	____	16.	______________________	________
____	____	____	17.	______________________	________
____	____	____	18.	______________________	________
____	____	____	19.	______________________	________
____	____	____	20.	______________________	________

Do you think you have a responsibility to save time? Explain. ______________________

____

____

____

What steps could you take to manage your time better? ______________________

____

____

Good and Poor Study Habits

Activity E
Chapter 18

Name ______________________________
Date _______________ **Period** _________

Identify each of the following study habits as good or poor. Then in the appropriate column, indicate how often you practice each habit by writing always, sometimes, or never.

Good Habits	Poor Habits	Study Habits
		1. Take notes in class.
		2. Take notes when you read assignments.
		3. Study in a cluttered area.
		4. Follow directions.
		5. Gather all the supplies you need before you start to study.
		6. Study in an area where you will be distracted.
		7. Set priorities for your time.
		8. Put off big assignments until the last day.
		9. Do all your studying the night before a test.
		10. Work in an area that is quiet and relaxing.
		11. Study and review the easy parts first.
		12. Do what must be done first.
		13. Study the tough parts last.
		14. Try to do two activities at the same time.
		15. Study when you are rested.
		16. Take a few moments after you study to think about what you studied.
		17. Study while watching TV.
		18. Do a little each day on big assignments that are due in a week or more.

Chapter 19
Communication Skills

Reinforcing Vocabulary

Activity A **Name** ______________________
Chapter 19 **Date** ______________ **Period** __________

Complete the following definitions by writing the missing term in the preceding blanks.

active listening	communicate	nonverbal
aggressive	complimentary	passive
assertive	feedback	public
body language	multitasking	verbal

______________ 1. Making speeches before audiences is known as _____ speaking.

______________ 2. A person with a(n) _____ communication style avoids conflict and usually has low self-esteem.

______________ 3. Listening and responding to improve mutual understanding is _____.

______________ 4. The sending and receiving of messages without the use of words is _____ communication.

______________ 5. A form of nonverbal communication in which messages are sent through body movements, facial expressions, and hand gestures is _____ _____.

______________ 6. A person with a(n) _____ communication style respects others while honestly expressing opinions and attitudes.

______________ 7. The return of information to the sender in order to check the accuracy of the communication is _____.

______________ 8. The type of communication involving the use of words is _____ communication.

______________ 9. Doing more than one job at a time is known as _____.

______________ 10. To share ideas, feelings, or information is to _____.

______________ 11. A person with a(n) _____ communication style achieves goals at the expense of others.

______________ 12. A phrase placed at the end of a letter, such as *sincerely* and *yours truly*, is a _____ close.

Speech Evaluation

Activity B **Name** ______________________
Chapter 19 **Date** ______________ **Period** __________

Using your own paper, write a two-minute speech on one of your favorite topics, such as a hobby, interest, or personal experience. Write notes for your speech on note cards and use them as you give your speech to the class. Then use the forms below to evaluate yourself and one classmate. Circle the numbers in the rating scale that best describe the speech presentations. Complete both forms and give the bottom one, unsigned, to your teacher.

Evaluating Yourself

Topic of speech:______________________

	Poor	Fair	Good	Very Good	Excellent
Had well-organized information:	1	2	3	4	5
Appeared calm and confident:	1	2	3	4	5
Showed enthusiasm:	1	2	3	4	5
Used proper grammar:	1	2	3	4	5
Spoke clearly:	1	2	3	4	5
Used varied tone of voice:	1	2	3	4	5
Spoke at good volume:	1	2	3	4	5
Spoke at good speed:	1	2	3	4	5
Kept good eye contact:	1	2	3	4	5
Had good posture:	1	2	3	4	5
Positive remarks:	1	2	3	4	5
Areas to improve next time:	1	2	3	4	5

Evaluating a Classmate

Evaluation of (name):______________________

Topic of speech:______________________

	Poor	Fair	Good	Very Good	Excellent
Had well-organized information:	1	2	3	4	5
Appeared calm and confident:	1	2	3	4	5
Showed enthusiasm:	1	2	3	4	5
Used proper grammar:	1	2	3	4	5
Spoke clearly:	1	2	3	4	5
Used varied tone of voice:	1	2	3	4	5
Spoke at good volume:	1	2	3	4	5
Spoke at good speed:	1	2	3	4	5
Kept good eye contact:	1	2	3	4	5
Had good posture:	1	2	3	4	5

Positive remarks: ______________________

Areas to improve next time: ______________________

Telephone Practice

Activity C
Chapter 19

Name ____________________
Date ______________ **Period** __________

Practice your telephone skills by completing the following exercises.

I. Receiving a Call

Imagine it is 12:10 p.m. on January 6 and you are in charge of answering the telephone at work. The caller, Bill Russell of Briswell Corporation, asks to speak with Maria Romero. Maria is on her lunch break. The caller wants to check an order he placed two weeks ago. His number is (609) 555-2232. Bill wants Maria to call him back. Use the form below to record this message.

To ____________________
Time ______________ Date ______________

While You Were OUT

M ____________________
of ____________________
Phone # ____________________

❑ Telephoned
❑ Came to see you
❑ Left the following message
❑ Please call back
❑ Will call again

____
____
____
____

II. Placing an Order

Imagine you work for Baxter Ford and your boss has asked you to call Bob Jensen at A to Z Parts Warehouse, (201) 555-0010, to place an order. You want three chrome handles for a 2001 Ford (part number A-1562-C) and two rear-seat speaker grills in black plastic (part number A-1378-BF). Your work phone number is (201) 555-1292. Your work address is 5937 Kingston Drive, Northern Springs, IN 52392. Plan your call by answering the following questions.

1. What company do you represent? ____________________
2. Who are you calling? ____________________
3. What telephone number are you calling? ____________________
4. Why are you calling? ____________________
5. What parts are you ordering? (Fill in the chart)

(Continued)

Name ______________________________

Part Description	Part Number	Color	Quantity
1.			
2.			

III. Making an Emergency Call

Imagine you work for Goodman Office Supplies, located at the corner of Brice and Bethel. One of the workers, Arnie Potter, just tripped over some boxes in the warehouse. He is lying on the floor, moaning in pain and holding his leg. Arnie is near retirement. He is in generally good health, but you know he suffers from high blood pressure. Role-play your telephone conversation for the class as you call for an ambulance.

Complete the following chart with the emergency phone numbers your family should have. Post a copy of this list near each phone in your home.

Emergency Phone Numbers

Fire ______________

Ambulance ______________

Gas Company ______________

Police ______________

Doctor ______________

Electric Company ______________

State Police ______________

Poison Control Center ______________

Water Company ______________

Others:

______________________________ ______________________________

______________________________ ______________________________

______________________________ ______________________________

______________________________ ______________________________

Remember, if you do not know what number to call in an emergency, just dial the operator.

Writing Business Letters

Activity D
Chapter 19

Name ____________________________
Date ______________ **Period** ________

Imagine you work for Edwards & Frederickson Financial Services. Your offices are located at 144 Grand Avenue, Centerville, NJ 08701. Your boss has asked you to help gather information about a new computer system. You are to write to Mr. Alvin J. Grant, president of Grant's Computer Company, 11 Lee Avenue, Southtown, NJ 04532, to request information about the new model BRX-527 computer system. You also need information about types of software packages available and those most suited for your office. Write your letter in the space below following the business letter format illustrated in the text.

Understanding Body Language

Activity E
Chapter 19

Name ______________________________
Date ________________ **Period** __________

Based on your first impression, write what you think each example of body language communicates. Then draw or describe three more examples of body language and tell what each communicates. Discuss your thoughts with others in class.

1. 
____

2. 
____

3. 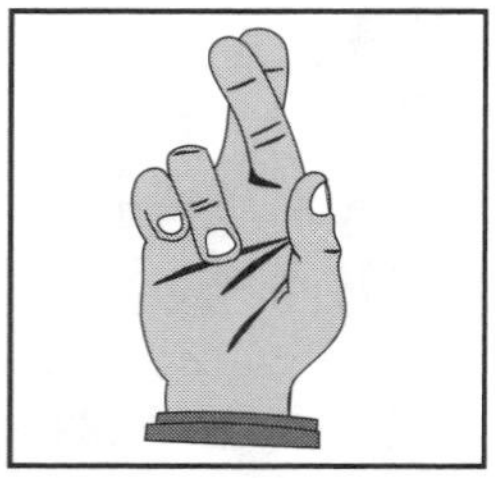
____

4. 
____

5. 
____

6. 
____

7. 
____

8. ______________________________

9. ______________________________

10. ______________________________

Chapter 20
Your Appearance

Reinforcing Vocabulary

Activity A **Name** ____________________
Chapter 20 **Date** ____________ **Period** ________

Match the following terms with their correct definitions.

_______ 1. Items that are popular for only a short period of time.
_______ 2. A skin disorder caused by inflammation of the skin glands and hair follicles.
_______ 3. Cleaning and caring for your body and clothes.
_______ 4. Items such as shoes, handbags, belts, neckties, and jewelry that are needed to complete outfits.
_______ 5. A set of rules that individuals must follow regarding clothing and general appearance.
_______ 6. A list of all the clothes and accessories you have in your closet and drawers.

A. accessories
B. acne
C. dress code
D. fads
E. grooming
F. wardrobe inventory

In the space below, write a paragraph or two about someone who is getting ready for work. Correctly use all the chapter terms listed above.

Check Your Grooming Habits

Activity B
Chapter 20

Name ____________________
Date ____________ **Period** ________

Answer the following questions by placing a check in the column that best describes your grooming habits.

	Always	Usually	Sometimes	Never
1. Do you keep your hair neat and clean?				
2. Do you shower or bathe daily?				
3. Do you use a deodorant or antiperspirant daily?				
4. Are your nails clean and well manicured?				
5. Do you brush and floss your teeth regularly?				
6. If you wear makeup, is it applied lightly for a natural look?				
7. If you wear fragrance, is it light and pleasant?				
8. Do you wear appropriate clothing to school?				
9. Do you wear appropriate clothing to work?				
10. If you wear jewelry, does it accent your clothing?				
11. Do your accessories coordinate with your clothing?				
12. Does your clothing fit properly?				
13. Do you wear clean clothing?				
14. Is your clothing free from wrinkles?				
15. Are your shoes clean or shined?				

What can you do to improve your grooming habits? ____________________

____

____

____

What Workers Wear

Activity C
Chapter 20

Name ______________________
Date ____________ **Period** ________

Make a list of all the clothing that you feel would be appropriate for each of the following workers.

Computer programmer:

____
____
____
____
____
____

Construction worker:

____
____
____
____
____
____

Bank teller:

____
____
____
____
____
____

Insurance salesperson:

____
____
____
____
____
____

Department store clerk:

____
____
____
____
____
____

Janitor:

____
____
____
____
____
____

List six occupations requiring a uniform.

______________________ ______________________
______________________ ______________________
______________________ ______________________

List six occupations for which your school clothes would be suitable.

______________________ ______________________
______________________ ______________________
______________________ ______________________

Wardrobe Planning for Work

Activity D
Chapter 20

Name ______________________
Date ____________ **Period** ________

You get the most from your clothing dollar when you carefully plan your wardrobe. Begin planning by listing the clothes you own that fit into each of the categories below. Then identify the job you would like to hold and make a complete list of the clothes you would need for it. Compare the clothes you need to what you already own. Then make a final list of clothing to buy for work.

School Clothes	Casual Clothes	Dressy Clothes

The job I would like to have is: ______________________

Work Clothes I Need	Work Clothes I Must Buy

Chapter 21
Good Health and Job Success

Reinforcing Vocabulary

Activity A **Name** ______________________

Chapter 21 **Date** ______________ **Period** __________

Complete the following definitions by writing the missing term in the preceding blanks.

addiction
balanced diet
drug
drug abuse
drug screening
nutrients
physical fitness
stress

______________ 1. A term that describes the reckless use of drugs is _____ _____.

______________ 2. A feeling of tension, strain, or pressure is _____.

______________ 3. The chemical substances in foods that nourish the body are _____.

______________ 4. An intake of food that supplies all the needed nutrients in the amounts needed to maintain good health is called a(n) _____ _____.

______________ 5. A(n) _____ is any chemical substance that brings about physical, emotional, or mental changes in people.

______________ 6. The ability to perform daily tasks easily with enough reserve energy to respond to unexpected demands is _____ _____.

______________ 7. The never-ending obsession to use a drug is called _____.

______________ 8. A test that can reveal the presence of drugs in a person's body is a _____ _____.

In the space below, write a paragraph or two about someone who knows the importance of good health to job success. Correctly use all the chapter terms listed above.

A Balanced Diet

Activity B **Name** ____________________
Chapter 21 **Date** ____________ **Period** ________

Jeff was hoping that he could make the basketball team next year. In order to do so, he knew he needed to be in excellent physical condition. Jeff had put on a few extra pounds from eating too much fast food and drinking too many sodas. He had heard about the MyPyramid.gov Web site you could use to find out what you should eat each day. He logged on and selected *MyPyramid Plan*. He entered the information requested—his age, gender, and activity level—and his personalized plan was created. It included the following recommendations for each day's food intake based on a 2800-calorie pattern:

Grains: 10 ounces
Vegetables: 3 ½ cups
Fruits: 2 ½ cups
Milk: 3 cups
Meat & beans: 7 ounces

Plan a day's menus for Jeff based on these recommendations. Be sure to include the correct amounts from each group in your sample menus. Also follow the recommendations of the Dietary Guidelines for Americans summarized in Figure 21-1 in your text.

Sample Daily Menus	
Breakfast	**Dinner**
Lunch	**Snacks**

Totals:

Grains: ____________ Fruits: ____________ Meat & beans: ____________

Vegetables: ____________ Milk: ____________

Learning About Stress

Activity C
Chapter 21

Name ______________________________

Date ________________ **Period** __________

Answer the following questions about how you view stress. Then, share your thoughts with a small group of classmates.

1. Place a check in the blank in front of each activity or situation you consider stressful.

____ A. going swimming
____ B. going on your first date
____ C. having a job interview
____ D. taking your driver's test
____ E. giving a speech
____ F. moving to a different town
____ G. playing softball
____ H. going on a picnic
____ I. starting a new job
____ J. reading a book
____ K. placing an order by telephone
____ L. training a new person at work
____ M. taking a surprise quiz

2. List three more activities you consider stressful.

A. ____

B. ____

C. ____

3. Place a check in the blank in front of each activity or situation that you feel helps reduce stress.

____ A. taking part in physical activities like jogging, bicycling, and swimming
____ B. having good eating and sleeping habits
____ C. drinking a lot of coffee and other drinks that contain caffeine
____ D. talking to someone about your problems
____ E. complaining about your problems
____ F. trying to get away from it all for a few minutes
____ G. planning the use of your time
____ H. being involved in civic or social groups
____ I. reading a book
____ J. playing a game
____ K. listening to music

4. List three of your own ideas for reducing stress.

A. ____

B. ____

C. ____

Avoiding Substance Abuse at Work

Activity D
Chapter 21

Name ______________________________
Date _______________ **Period** __________

Imagine you are an employer. Answer the following questions related to tobacco, alcohol, and drug use in your company.

1. What would your employee handbook say regarding your policy on smoking? ____________________

2. What would be the advantages of having a smoke-free workplace? ____________________

3. How would you help an employee who wanted to quit smoking? ____________________

4. What would your employee handbook say regarding your drug and alcohol policy? ____________________

5. What would be the advantages of having an alcohol- and drug-free workplace? ____________________

6. How would you help an employee who had an alcohol or drug problem? ____________________

Chapter 22
Developing Leadership Skills

Reinforcing Vocabulary

Activity A
Chapter 22

Name ____________________
Date ____________ **Period** ________

Match the following terms with their correct definitions.

_______ 1. A person who influences the actions of others.
_______ 2. The president, vice president, secretary, and treasurer of a student organization.
_______ 3. The most common reference used in parliamentary law.
_______ 4. A list of activities that will occur during a meeting.
_______ 5. An orderly way of conducting a meeting and discussing group business.
_______ 6. The person who usually conducts a group's meetings.
_______ 7. Groups that help students develop leadership skills and prepare to work in certain occupational areas.
_______ 8. The ability to lead or direct others on a course or in a direction.
_______ 9. A group within an organization that handles a specific function of the organization's work.
_______ 10. Something members of career/technical student organizations share.

A. agenda
B. career goals
C. career/technical student organization
D. committee
E. leader
F. leadership
G. officers
H. parliamentary procedure
I. president
J. Robert's Rules of Order

Being a Good Leader

Activity B **Name** ____________________________
Chapter 22 **Date** ______________ **Period** __________

Describe how a leader could demonstrate each leadership trait listed. You may use examples from your own experiences or create new ones.

1. A good leader respects other people. Example: ______________________________

2. A good leader accepts responsibility and works within the group. Example: ______________________________

3. A good leader gets along with others in a friendly and peaceful manner. Example: ______________________________

4. A good leader gives praise where praise is due. Example: ______________________________

5. A good leader communicates thoughts and feelings in a clear and understandable manner. Example: ______________________________

6. A good leader is well informed on matters that concern the group. Example: ______________________________

7. A good leader is confident and honest. Example: ______________________________

8. A good leader is positive and excited about the group's goals. Example: ______________________________

9. A good leader is open-minded and can help set group goals. Example: ______________________________

10. A good leader can get the group started and keep it on track. Example: ______________________________

Learning About Career/Technical Student Organizations

Activity C
Chapter 22

Name ______________________________

Date ____________________ **Period** __________

The chart below lists some of the larger state and national career/technical student organizations. Write a brief description of each organization and list the classes that you feel relate to each organization.

Organization	Description of Organization	Classes That Relate
1. Business Professionals of America (BPA)		
2. DECA—An Association of Marketing Students		
3. Family, Career, and Community Leaders of America (FCCLA)		
4. Future Business Leaders of America—Phi Beta Lambda (FBLA-PBL)		
5. Health Occupations Students of America (HOSA)		
6. National FFA Organization (FFA)		
7. SkillsUSA		
8. Technology Student Association (TSA)		

Which organizations described above interest you? Why?

____

____

____

____

Your Career-Related CTSO

Activity D **Name** ______________________

Chapter 22 **Date** ____________ **Period** ________

Research a career/technical student organization to which you belong or would like to join. Then answer the following questions.

1. What career/technical student organizations are in your school? ______________________

2. Which career/technical student organization is best suited to your interests and needs? ______________________

3. Write the motto of this organization. ______________________

4. What is the purpose of the organization? ______________________

5. What are the colors of the organization? What does each of the colors mean? ______________________

6. Describe the symbol of the organization. ______________________

7. What are the parts of the symbol and what do they mean? ______________________

8. Describe the official dress of the organization. ______________________

Chapter 23
Paychecks and Taxes

Reinforcing Vocabulary

Activity A **Name** ______________________________
Chapter 23 **Date** _______________ **Period** __________

Match the following terms with their correct definitions.

________ 1. A length of time for which an employee's wages are calculated. Most businesses have weekly, biweekly, semimonthly, or monthly pay periods.

________ 2. The total amount of money earned during a pay period.

________ 3. The amount of money left after all deductions have been taken from the gross pay.

________ 4. Employee's withholding allowance certificate; a form filled out by an employee when beginning a new job. It determines how much of the employee's pay should be withheld for taxes.

________ 5. A person, such as a child or nonworking adult, who relies on a taxpayer for financial support.

________ 6. Wage and tax statement; a form showing how much a worker was paid and how much income was withheld for taxes in a given year.

________ 7. The agency that enforces federal tax laws and collects taxes.

________ 8. A tax on all forms of earnings.

________ 9. An act that allows the federal government to reserve a percentage of a paycheck for social security tax.

A. dependent
B. Federal Insurance Contributions Act (FICA)
C. Form W-2
D. Form W-4
E. gross pay
F. income tax
G. Internal Revenue Service (IRS)
H. net pay
I. pay period

Reading a Paycheck Stub

Activity B **Name** ______________________
Chapter 23 **Date** ______________ **Period** ________

Use the paycheck stub shown below to answer the questions that follow.

1. What is Sarah's hourly wage? ______________________
2. How many hours did Sarah work last week? ______________________
3. What is Sarah's gross pay for this pay period? ______________________
4. How much was withheld from Sarah's gross pay for Federal income tax? ______________________
5. How much was withheld from Sarah's gross pay for Social Security tax? ______________________
6. What are Sarah's gross earnings so far this year? ______________________
7. How much state income tax has been withheld from Sarah's paycheck so far this year? ______________________
8. What is Sarah's net pay for this pay period? ______________________
9. If Sarah works 15 hours next week, what will her gross pay be? ______________________
10. What will Sarah's year to date earnings total after working 15 hours next week? ______________________

REGULAR RATE	REGULAR HOURS	OTHER HOURS	REGULAR EARNINGS	OTHER EARNINGS	TAXABLE ADJUSTMENT	NONTAXABLE ADJUSTMENT	TAXABLE GROSS EARNINGS
12.70	23.00		292.10				292.10

DEDUCTIONS

TOTAL EARNINGS	FED W/H TAX	FICA	STATE TAX	LOCAL TAX	MEDICARE
292.10	34.92	20.88	5.96		4.24

YEAR TO DATE TOTALS

EARNINGS	FED W/H TAX	FICA	STATE TAX	LOCAL TAX	MEDICARE
2471.17	295.42	1726.64	50.42		35.87

OTHER DEDUCTIONS

		INS						

123-45-6789	Sarah E. Goldberg

CHECK NO.	PERIOD ENDING	NET PAY
47503	3/16/XX	226.10

DETACH AND RETAIN THIS STUB FOR YOUR RECORDS

Your Tax Dollars at Work

Activity C
Chapter 23

Name ______________________________
Date ______________ **Period** __________

Prepare a list of 10 questions for local and state government officials regarding how tax dollars are spent. Meet with the officials in person, write them a letter, or send questions via e-mail. Write your questions in the space provided. On the following page, write an article summarizing the answers to your questions.

Official(s) interviewed: ______________________________

____

Method(s) of contacting official(s):______________________________

____

1. ______________________________
2. ______________________________
3. ______________________________
4. ______________________________
5. ______________________________
6. ______________________________
7. ______________________________
8. ______________________________
9. ______________________________
10. ______________________________

(Continued)

Name ______________________________

Your Tax Dollars at Work

Chapter 24
Budgets

Reinforcing Vocabulary

Activity A
Chapter 24

Name ______________________________
Date ____________________ **Period** ___________

Read each of the incomplete definitions below and decide which chapter term is being defined. Write the correct terms in the crossword puzzle.

Across

2. A ______ expense involves a set amount of money due on a set date.
3. ______ expenses are paid four times a year.
6. ______ expenses are paid once a year.

Down

1. ______ expenses are paid twice a year.
4. A ______ is a plan for the use or management of money.
5. ______ expenses vary in amount.

Fixed and Flexible Expenses

Activity B
Chapter 24

Name ______________________________
Date ________________ **Period** __________

Read the list of expenses below and decide whether each expense listed is fixed or flexible. List each expense in the appropriate column of the chart.

Movie tickets
Rent payments
Gasoline
Jewelry
New shoes
Mortgage payments
Makeup
Automobile maintenance
Amusement park tickets
Telephone bills
Loan payments
Laundry
Books and magazines
Ice cream
Auto insurance
Automobile loan payments
Birthday presents
Savings

Fixed Expenses	Flexible Expenses

Making Your Money Work for You

Activity C
Chapter 24

Name ______________________________
Date ______________ **Period** __________

Answer the following questions to help you evaluate your purchase goals before planning a budget.

1. What are your current sources of income? ____

2. Identify three items you want to buy within a year and list them below in the *now* column. Also list three long-range purchases you want to buy in the *later* column. Use catalogs or newspaper ads to help you estimate the cost of the six items. Total each column.

	Now	**Cost**	**Later**	**Cost**
A.	______________	$______	______________	$______
B.	______________	$______	______________	$______
C.	______________	$______	______________	$______
	Total	**$**______	**Total**	**$**______

3. Will you be able to afford the items in your *now* column in a year or less? __________

   If yes, what is your next short-term purchase goal? ____

   If no, how could you increase your income? ____

4. Are you currently saving any of your income? ____

   If yes, what are your plans for the money you are saving? ____

   If no, how could you adjust your current spending pattern to start saving? ____

5. How can saving now help you reach some of your long-term purchase goals? ____

Planning a Budget

Activity D
Chapter 24

Name ____________________
Date ____________ **Period** __________

Complete this form to develop a one-month budget for the lifestyle you desire. Include dollar amounts for the categories of spending that would apply to you.

Monthly Budgeting Plan

Estimated Income	
Net income (wages)	______
Tips	______
Other	______
Total	$ ______
Estimated Fixed Expenses	
Housing	
Rent or mortgage payments	______
Maintenance fees	______
Monthly cable service	______
Monthly Internet service	______
Other	______
Insurance Premiums	
Life	______
Health/medical	______
Automobile	______
Home	______
Other	______
Debts and Obligations	
Automobile loan payments	______
Other installment loan payments	______
Contributions	______
Tuition	______
Membership dues	______
Other	______
Other	______
Other	______
Taxes and Licenses	
Property taxes	______
Automobile license plates	______
Other	______
Total	$ ______

Estimated Flexible Expenses	
Food	
At home	______
Away from home	______
Clothing and Accessories	
New clothes	______
Cleaning and laundry	______
Accessories	______
Grooming aids	______
Household	
Home furnishings	______
Maintenance and repair	______
Gas	______
Electricity	______
Water	______
Telephone	______
Transportation	
Gasoline	______
Automobile maintenance	______
Public transportation	______
Medical Needs	
Doctor	______
Dentist	______
Other	______
Savings	
Savings account	______
Investment/retirement account	______
Other	______
Recreation and Entertainment	
Movies	______
Vacations	______
Sport events	______
Books and magazines	______
Other	______
Total	$ ______

Summary

Total estimated income	$ ______
Total estimated expenses ($______ fixed + $______ flexible)	– ______
Balance (income minus expenses)	$ ______

If you would have a positive balance (income greater than expenses), what would you do with the extra money? ____________________

If you would have a negative balance (income less than expenses), how would you adjust your income or expenses to have a workable budget? ____________________

Chapter 25
Checking Accounts

Reinforcing Vocabulary

Activity A
Chapter 25

Name ______________________
Date ____________ **Period** ________

Match the following terms with their correct definitions.

_______ 1. Is used to record how much money you put in your account.
_______ 2. A written order to pay someone.
_______ 3. To sign your name on the back of a check made out to you so you can cash it.
_______ 4. To write checks for more money than you have.
_______ 5. A list of your deposits, withdrawals (in the form of checks), service charges, and interest payments.
_______ 6. An item that guarantees payment; used by a bank to withdraw the requested amount from a checking account.
_______ 7. An item drawn by the bank on its own funds.
_______ 8. An item that is an order to pay a certain amount of money to a certain party.
_______ 9. Items purchased to avoid taking cash on vacation.
_______ 10. Combines the functions of a check and an ATM card.

A. bank statement
B. cashier's check
C. certified check
D. check
E. debit card
F. deposit slip
G. endorse
H. money order
I. overdraw
J. traveler's checks

Identifying Parts of a Check

Activity B **Name** ____________________
Chapter 25 **Date** ____________ **Period** ________

Examine the check below. On the next page, identify each of the numbered parts as indicated. Then give a brief description of each.

account number	check number	name and address
account open date	date	pay to the order of
amount in numbers	fractional routing number	routing number
amount in words	memo	signature

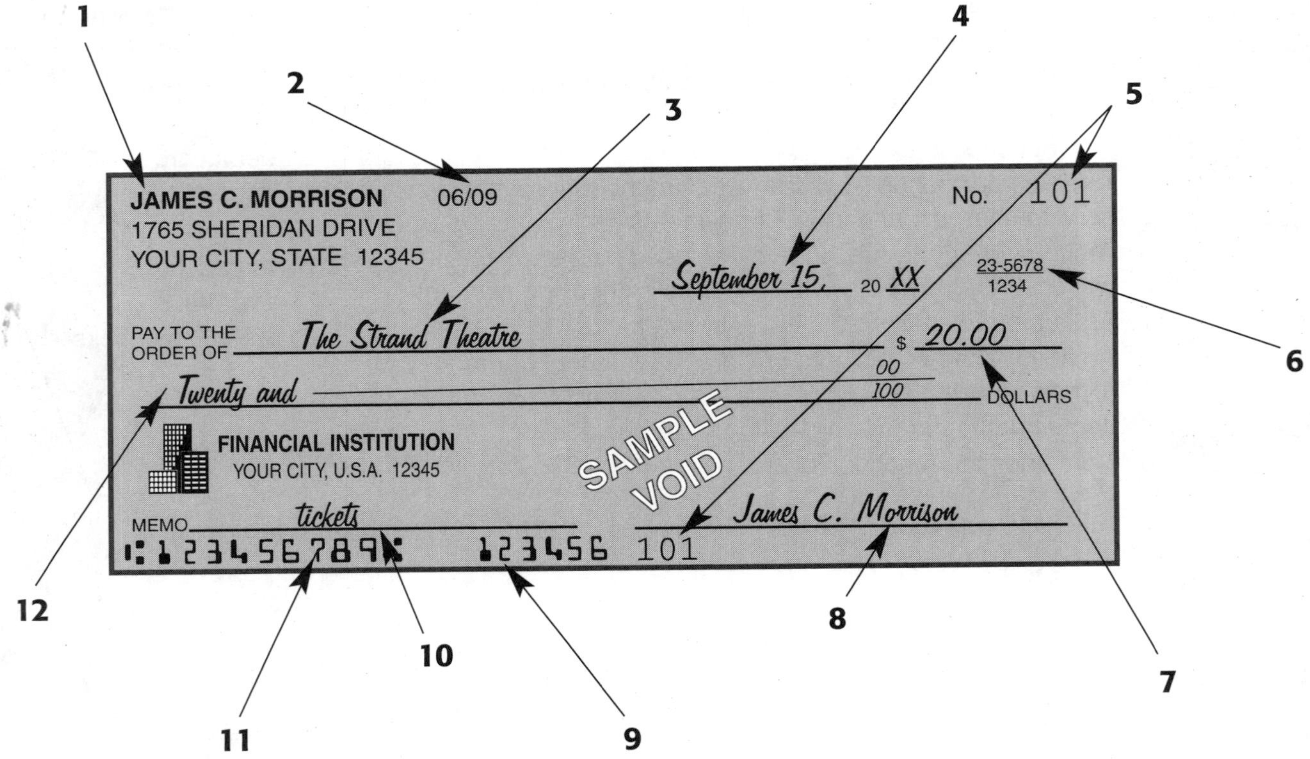

(Continued)

Check part:	Description:
1.	
2.	
3.	
4.	
5.	
6.	
7.	
8.	
9.	
10.	
11.	
12.	

Using a Checking Account

Activity C | **Name** ______________________________
Chapter 25 | **Date** _______________ **Period** __________

With the information below, practice writing checks, completing a deposit slip, and filling in a check register. The checks should be dated for October of the current year. Provide your name and address in the top left corners of the checks and the deposit slip. Your beginning balance is $150.10.

Check Number	Date	Transaction	
102	10/5	Shop Rite (groceries)	$50.00
103	10/11	Sears (charge account #23596)	$44.20
104	10/20	Easy Life Insurance Co.	$36.50
	10/21	Deposit (Check 16-214)	$250.00

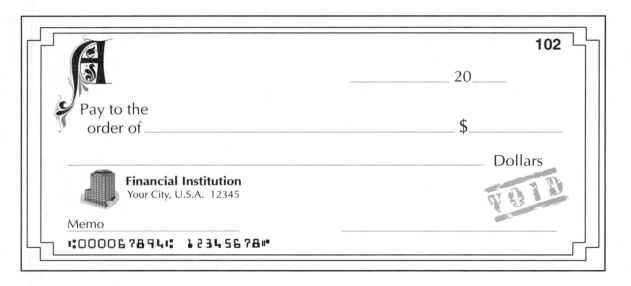

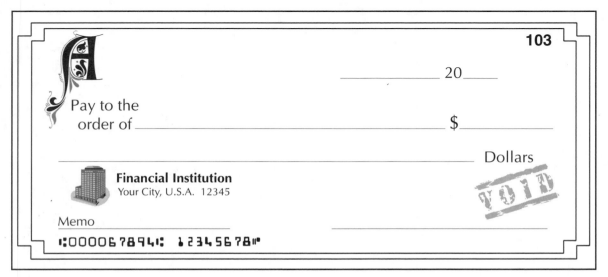

102

_______________ 20_____

Pay to the order of ______________________________ $__________

______________________________ Dollars

Financial Institution
Your City, U.S.A. 12345

VOID

Memo ____________________ ____________________

⑆000067894⑆ 12345678⑈

103

_______________ 20_____

Pay to the order of ______________________________ $__________

______________________________ Dollars

Financial Institution
Your City, U.S.A. 12345

VOID

Memo ____________________ ____________________

⑆000067894⑆ 12345678⑈

(Continued)

Name ____________________

104

________ 20____

Pay to the order of ______________________ $________

______________________ Dollars

Financial Institution
Your City, U.S.A. 12345

VOID

Memo ____________ ____________

⑆000067894⑆ 12345678⑈

DEPOSIT

Name ____________________

Date ____________ 20____

____

Financial Institution
Your City, U.S.A. 12345

CASH	CURRENCY		
	COIN		
CHECKS			
TOTAL FROM OTHER SIDE			
TOTAL			
LESS CASH RECEIVED			
NET DEPOSIT			

00-6789/0000

USE OTHER SIDE FOR ADDITIONAL LISTING

BE SURE EACH ITEM IS PROPERLY ENDORSED

⑆000067894⑆ 12345678⑈

ALL ITEMS ARE ACCEPTED SUBJECT TO OUR RULES AND REGULATIONS APPLICABLE TO THIS ACCOUNT

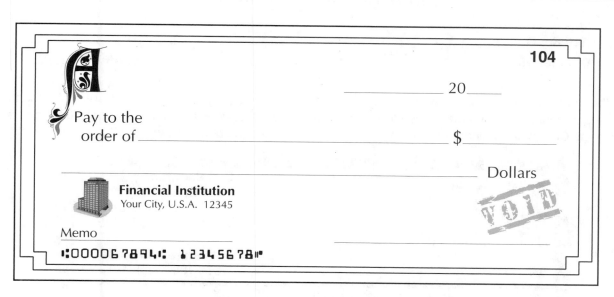

RECORD ALL CHARGES OR CREDITS THAT AFFECT YOUR ACCOUNT

NUMBER	DATE	DESCRIPTION OF TRANSACTION	PAYMENT/DEBIT (–)	√ T	FEE (IF ANY) (–)	DEPOSIT/CREDIT (+)	BALANCE $
			$		$	$	

REMEMBER TO RECORD AUTOMATIC PAYMENTS / DEPOSITS ON DATE AUTHORIZED.

Balancing a Checkbook

Activity D **Name** ______________________________
Chapter 25 **Date** ________________ **Period** __________

Use the bank statement below and the check register on the next page to help Peter Banks balance his checking account. On the register, use the check (✓) column to check off items that appear on the bank statement. Complete the last form to make sure Peter's checkbook balances with his bank statement.

FI
Financial Institution

Statement for
Peter Banks
222 Atlantic Avenue
Toms River, NJ 58625

This statement covers
1/01/XX through 1/31/XX

Checking Account 123-4567	**Previous Statement Balance On** 12/31/XX		525.10
	Total of 2 **Deposits for**		2050.00+
	Total of 4 **Withdrawals for**		410.00-
	Total Interest Earned		0
	Total Service Charges		10.00
	New Balance		2155.10
Checks and Other Debits	**Check/Debit**	**Date Paid**	**Amount**
	ATM Withdrawl #00284	1/6	30.00
	Debit Card Withdrawl #33956 Foodsaver	1/17	95.00
	501	1/19	35.00
	Automatic transfer to account #09876543	1/30	250.00
Deposits and Other Credits		**Date Posted**	**Amount**
	Direct Deposit from #08549 on 1/11	1/11	1025.00
	Direct Deposit from #08549 on 1/25	1/25	1025.00

Thank you for banking with Your Financial Institution

(Continued)

Name ______________________________

AS–Automatic Deposit	AP–Automatic Payment	DC–Debit Card					
NUMBER OR CODE	**DATE**	**DESCRIPTION OF TRANSACTION**	**PAYMENT/DEBIT (–)**	**√ T**	**FEE (IF ANY) (–)**	**DEPOSIT/CREDIT (+)**	**BALANCE** $ 525 10
DC	1/6	Cash	$ 30 00		$	$	30 00 495 10
AD	1/11	Deposit				1025 00	1025 00 1520 10
501	1/16	T.J. Garage (Oil and lube)	35 00				35 00 1485 10
DC	1/17	Foodsaver (Groceries)	95 00				95 00 1390 10
AD	1/25	Deposit				1025 00	1025 00 2415 10
502	1/29	Pleasant Hill Apartment (February rent)	700 00				700 00 1715 10
AP	1/30	Tranfer to Savings	250 00				250 00 1465 10
503	2/1	Medical Associates (Office visit co-pay)	30 00				30 00 1435 10
504	2/3	Telephone Company (January phone bill)	41 75				41 75 1393 35
	2/5	Deposit (birthday gift)				25 00	25 00 1418 35

OUTSTANDING CHECKS	
Check No.	Amount
TOTAL	

Enter statement balance	
List deposits not credited on this statement and add to statement balance.	
Subtotal	
Subtract checks outstanding	
TOTAL	

Enter current checkbook balance	
Add any interest shown on statement	
Subtract any charges shown on statement	
New checkbook balance	

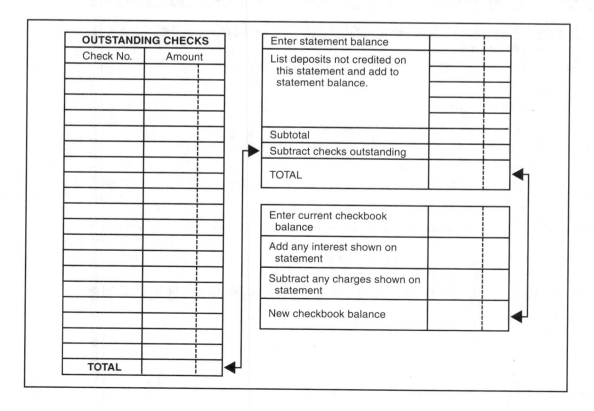

Correcting an Imbalance

Activity E | **Name** ____________________
Chapter 25 | **Date** ______________ **Period** ________

Karen's checkbook register does not balance with her bank statement. Check to make sure that Karen did not make any math errors in her register. Write the numbers that should appear in the balance column in the spaces provided beside the checkbook register. Then answer the following questions.

AS–Automatic Deposit   AP–Automatic Payment   DC–Debit Card

NUMBER OR CODE	DATE	DESCRIPTION OF TRANSACTION	PAYMENT/DEBIT (−) $		√ T	FEE (IF ANY) (−) $	DEPOSIT/CREDIT (+) $		BALANCE $		
									635	00	
AP	2/3	Harrison's Motors	235	00					235	00	
		(Car payment)							400	00	1. ________
207	2/7	Cindy Wright	25	00					25	00	
		(Birthday present)							375	00	2. ________
AD	2/7	Deposit					980	65	980	65	
									1355	65	3. ________
208	2/9	City Utilities	63	69					63	69	
		(January bill)							1293	66	4. ________
209	2/11	ABC Wireless	52	10					52	10	
		(Cell phone bill)							1241	56	5. ________
DC	2/19	Exclusive Clothier	152	68					152	68	
		(party dress)							1088	88	6. ________
AD	2/21	Deposit					981	65	981	65	
									2070	53	7. ________
211	2/25	Skyview Apartments					695	00	695	00	
		(March rent)							1375	53	8. ________

	Check/Debit	Date Paid	Amount
Checks and Other Debits	Automatic payment #04882 Harrison's Motors	2/3	235.00
	207	2/11	25.00
	ATM Withdrawl #77025	2/13	40.00
	Service Charge — ATM Withdrawl #77025	2/13	2.00
	208	2/14	63.69
	209	2/16	52.10
	Debit Card Withdrawl #79623 Exclusive Clothier	2/19	152.68
	210	2/23	59.70
	211	2/28	695.00
		Date Posted	**Amount**
Deposits and Other Credits	Direct Deposit from #09384 on 2/7	2/7	980.65
	Direct Deposit from #024731 on 2/21	2/21	981.65

9. Besides math errors, what other mistakes did Karen make? ____
____
____

10. What should the balance in Karen's register now read? ____
____

Chapter 26
Savings

Reinforcing Vocabulary

Activity A — **Name** ______________________
Chapter 26 — **Date** ______________ **Period** __________

Complete the following definitions by writing the missing term in the preceding blanks.

annual percentage yield	money market account
annuity	mutual fund
certificates of deposit	principal
compound interest	savings club
direct deposit	U.S. savings bonds
interest	

______________________ 1. A _____ _____ is a long-term investment that provides a way to invest in stocks and bonds.

______________________ 2. Money paid to you for allowing a financial institution to use your money is known as _____.

______________________ 3. The _____ is the amount of your original deposit in an account.

______________________ 4. Interest that is earned on both the principal and the earned interest is _____ _____.

______________________ 5. An account into which you deposit a set amount of money every week or month is called a(n) _____ _____.

______________________ 6. _____ _____ _____ are purchased for a certain amount of money and are held for a set period of time.

______________________ 7 The _____ _____ _____ is the rate (or percent) of yearly earnings from an account.

______________________ 8. _____ _____ _____ are certificates of debt issued by the federal government.

______________________ 9. _____ _____ is a program that allows your employer to deposit your paycheck directly into your account.

______________________ 10. An account that is similar to a CD but has no time period restrictions is called a(n) _____ _____ _____.

______________________ 11. A(n) _____ is a form of investment that provides insurance as well as savings.

Financial Institutions

Activity B **Name** ______________________________
Chapter 26 **Date** ____________________ **Period** __________

Obtain brochures describing a commercial bank, savings bank, and credit union and the services they offer. Complete the chart with the information you learn about each. Then answer the questions below.

Commercial Bank	Savings Bank	Credit Union
Name:	Name:	Name:
Location:	Location:	Location:
Hours:	Hours:	Hours:
Interest on savings accounts:	Interest on savings accounts:	Interest on savings accounts:
Interest on checking accounts:	Interest on checking accounts:	Interest on checking accounts:
Services offered:	Services offered:	Services offered:
Minimum balance required:	Minimum balance required:	Minimum balance required:
Fees:	Fees:	Fees:

In what ways are these financial institutions similar? ______________________________

____

____

____

____

In what ways are these financial institutions different? ______________________________

____

____

____

____

If you were opening a new savings account, would you choose one of these institutions or an Internet bank? Explain. ____

____

____

____

Savings Deposits and Withdrawals

Activity C
Chapter 26

Name ____________________
Date ______________ **Period** __________

Use your name, today's date, and the information below to complete the deposit slip and withdrawal slip.

With the deposit slip, you want to receive a $50 bill after making the following deposit:

bills—three twenties, one ten, and three singles

coins—160 quarters, 100 dimes, 40 nickels, and 300 pennies

checks—#14-610 for $32.10 and #70-7211 for $43.83

With your withdrawal slip, you want to withdraw $40 from your account.

SAVINGS DEPOSIT

Name ____________________

Date ______________ 20____

____

CASH	CURRENCY		
	COIN		
CHECKS			
TOTAL FROM OTHER SIDE			
TOTAL			
LESS CASH RECEIVED			
NET DEPOSIT			

00-6789/0000

USE OTHER SIDE FOR ADDITIONAL LISTING

BE SURE EACH ITEM IS PROPERLY ENDORSED

Financial Institution
Your City, U.S.A. 12345

⑆000067894⑆ 12345678⑈

ALL ITEMS ARE ACCEPTED SUBJECT TO OUR RULES AND REGULATIONS APPLICABLE TO THIS ACCOUNT

SAVINGS WITHDRAWAL

MUST BE PRESENTED BY THE SAVINGS CUSTOMER IN PERSON OR BY MAIL.

00-6789/0000

Name ____________________ ACCOUNT NO. ______________
PLEASE TYPE OR PRINT CLEARLY

______________ 20____

____________________ Dollars $ ____________

DEDUCT ABOVE SUM FROM MY SAVINGS ACCOUNT ON DEPOSIT WITH:

Financial Institution
Your City, U.S.A. 12345

SIGN HERE ____________________

How Your Money Grows

Activity D Name ____________
Chapter 26 Date ____________ Period ________

Use the chart below to answer the following questions about the power of compounding.

How $10 Can Grow				
Year	**Rate of Interest (compounded monthly)**			
	5%	**7%**	**10%**	**12%**
1	$123	$125	$127	$128
2	253	258	267	272
3	389	402	421	435
4	532	555	592	618
5	683	720	781	825
6	841	897	989	1058
7	1,008	1,086	1,220	1,320
8	1,182	1,289	1,474	1,615
9	1,366	1,507	1,755	1,948
10	1,559	1,741	2,066	2,323
15	2,684	3,188	4,179	5,046
20	4,128	5,240	7,657	9,991
25	5,980	8,148	13,379	18,976

Note: The chart shows monthly contributions of $10 with a return of 5%, 7%, 10%, and 12% compounded monthly for up to 25 years (figures have been rounded).

1. Determine how much your savings would be worth in 5 years if you contribute $10 a month at the following interest rates:
   A. 5% ____________
   B. 7% ____________
   C. 10% ____________
2. Why is it wise to compare interest rates before opening a savings account? ____________
3. Assume you invest $10 a month in an account with a 12% interest rate.
   A. What will your investment be worth in 25 years? ____________
   B. How much money will you have contributed? ____________
   C. How much of the account's value is due to interest? ____________

(Continued)

Name ______________________________

4. How can compounding help you reach your long-term savings goals? ______________________________

5. If Henri saves $10 a month, earning 10% interest, how much will he have saved in six years? ______

6. Tia just celebrated her 25th birthday. If Tia saves $10 a month, earning 10% interest, how much will she have saved by age 50? ______________________________

7. How much more savings will Tia have than Henri? ______________________________

8. T.J. would like to start saving for a cruise vacation. He estimates that he will need at least $1,000 for his trip.

   A. If he opens a savings account that earns a 7% rate of interest and saves $10 a month, how many years will it take to reach his goal? ______________________________

   B. How could T.J. reach his goal more quickly? ______________________________

9. Brittany contributes $10 each month to her savings account. She currently has $1,755 in her account.

   A. Using the chart, determine the number of years that Brittany has been contributing to her account.

   ____

   B. What is the interest rate on her account? ______________________________

10. Develop a savings plan for one of your long-term savings goals. Include the monthly contribution, interest rate, and number of years needed to reach your goal. ______________________________

Savings Survey

Activity E
Chapter 26

Name ____________________
Date __________ **Period** ______

If you have a savings account, answer the following questions based on your savings experience. If you do not have a savings account, use these questions to interview someone who does. Compare your answers with others in class.

1. Is saving money important to you? Explain. ____________________
____
____

2. Rank the following reasons for saving in order of their importance to you—from 1 (most important) to 7 (least important).
   ____ emergencies
   ____ future income reduction
   ____ travel and recreation
   ____ advanced education
   ____ major purchases, such as a car or home
   ____ retirement
   ____ overall financial security

3. Aside from the seven reasons listed above, what other reasons do you have for saving money? ______
____

4. What are the advantages to saving money in a financial institution instead of at home? ______
____

5. What type of savings account do you have? ____________________
6. In what type of financial institution is your savings account? ____________________
7. What interest rate does your savings account earn? ____________________
8. How often is interest paid on your savings? ____________________
9. How often do you make deposits into your savings? ____________________
10. How often do you withdraw money from your savings? ____________________
11. Do you have more than one savings account? If so, describe your other account(s) in terms of the information included in Questions 5 through 10. ____________________
____
____
____

12. Besides a savings account, what other financial services offered by your financial institution have you used? ____________________
____

13. What advice would you give to someone who is considering opening a savings account? ______
____

Chapter 27 Credit

Reinforcing Vocabulary

Activity A
Chapter 27

Name ____________________
Date ______________ **Period** __________

Read each of the definitions below and decide which chapter term is being defined. Write the correct terms in the crossword puzzle.

Across

1. The maximum amount a person can charge.
4. Valuable possessions you own, money you have in bank accounts, and the value of stocks and bonds you own are examples.
5. A type of theft that occurs when someone uses your personal information, such as your name, social security number, or credit card number without your permission to commit fraud or other crimes.
6. Contracts that legally bind a lender and a borrower to credit terms described in writing.
7. Someone who guarantees that your loan will be paid and must make the payments if you do not.

Down

1. Organizations that check credit applications and gather financial information on people to help businesses decide whether to grant or deny people credit.
2. An estimate of how likely you are to repay your bills on time.
3. Something of value held by a lending institution in case you fail to repay.

Credit Advantages and Disadvantages

Activity B **Name** ______________________
Chapter 27 **Date** ______________ **Period** __________

Read each statement. Write an *A* in the blank if the statement is an advantage of using credit. Write a *D* for each disadvantage of using credit. Then follow the directions below.

_______ 1. Credit is a convenience.
_______ 2. Credit encourages impulse buying.
_______ 3. Credit allows you to use goods and services while paying for them.
_______ 4. Credit helps you meet financial emergencies.
_______ 5. Credit ties up your future income.
_______ 6. Credit makes the costs of goods and services higher.
_______ 7. Credit can get you into serious debt.
_______ 8. Credit can cause you to overspend.
_______ 9. Credit allows you to shop and travel without the worry of carrying large amounts of cash.
_______ 10. Credit spreads out the cost of expensive items over a period of time.

Describe a real or fictitious situation in which a person uses credit wisely.

Describe a real or fictitious situation in which a person abuses credit and is harmed by the misuse.

For what types of items would you use credit?

For what types of items would you avoid using credit?

The Cost of Credit

Activity C
Chapter 27

Name ______________________________
Date ______________ **Period** __________

Complete the following exercises to figure the cost of using various types of credit.

Credit Cards

Your credit card balance for this month is $60. You can pay the full balance or make a minimum payment of $10 each month. If you choose to make the minimum payment, you will be charged 1.5 percent interest per month (18 percent annual interest) on the unpaid balance. The steps below show how to figure the cost of carrying an unpaid balance.

Step 1: Subtract the minimum payment from the total balance to get the remaining balance.

$60.00 – 10.00 = $50.00

Step 2: Multiply the remaining balance by the interest rate (.015). This is the cost of delaying full payment for another month.

$50.00 × .015 = $ 0.75

Step 3: Add the answers to steps one and two to find the new balance that will appear on next month's bill. Use this figure to begin the calculations for next month (Month 2).

$50.00 + .75 = $50.75

Figure the total cost of making minimum payments until the bill is paid off by repeating the above steps.

Month 2:

Step 1: $50.75 – 10.00 = $________

Step 2: $ ________ × .015 = $________

Step 3: $ ________ + ________ = $________

Month 3:

Step 1: $________ – 10.00 = $________

Step 2: $________ × .015 = $________

Step 3: $ ________ + ________ = $________

Month 4:

Step 1: $________ – 10.00 = $________

Step 2: $________ × .015 = $________

Step 3: $ ________ + ________ = $________

Month 5:

Step 1: $________ – 10.00 = $________

Step 2: $________ × .015 = $________

Step 3: $ ________ + ________ = $________

Month 6:

Pay remaining balance in full at this time. $________

Add together the six monthly payments. $________

Then subtract the original total balance from this sum. What was the total cost of delaying full payment on this credit card bill? $________

Installment Credit

The cash price of a television is $600.00. However, you can purchase it on credit by paying $100.00 cash now and $46.67 monthly for one year.

Step 1: Multiply the amount of each payment by the number of payments.

$________ × ________ = $________

Step 2: Add the cash payment to the answer in step 1. This is the total cost of the television.

$________ + ________ = $________

Step 3: Subtract the cash price from the answer to step 2. This is the cost of using credit.

$________ – ________ = $________

The Credit Game

Activity D
Chapter 27

Name ______________________________
Date ____________________ **Period** ____________

Evaluate your credit history as you play the game below with two or three of your classmates. Use buttons or circles of paper for markers. Take turns flipping a coin to move around the board. If the coin is flipped "heads," move the marker two spaces. If the coin is flipped "tails," move the marker one space. The player who finishes first is the winner.

1.
Start

2.
Your savings account shows a steady pattern of saving over the last three years. Move ahead 1 space.

3.

4.
Your charge accounts with the local gas and electric companies show that you frequently pay late fees. Move back 1 space.

5.
You just got a job! Your steady source of income makes you a good credit risk. Take another turn.

6.
Someone has stolen your credit card and other identity information and has made fraudulent purchases. Miss one turn to get the matter resolved.

7.
You are already spending 20 percent of your take-home pay on installment debts. You cannot afford any more credit. Go back to start.

8.

9.
You pay the total due on your gasoline credit card on time each month. Move ahead 2 spaces.

10.
Your credit cards are always charged to the limit and you've carried a large unpaid balance for the last 15 months. Miss a turn while you pay off some of your debt.

11.

12.
You purchased a new TV on installment credit. You failed to make your payments and the set was repossessed. Move back 1 space.

13.
You've repaid a loan to your company credit union in a timely fashion. Take another turn.

14.

15.
Your loan fell through because the credit bureau said that your cosigner has a worse credit history than you do. Move back to space #10.

16.
You have a reputation for making payments on time at a local department store. Move ahead 1 space.

17.

18.
Easy credit has caused you to fall into a pattern of impulse buying. Miss a turn to give yourself time to plan your next purchases.

19.

20.
Congratulations! You've shown that you can manage money responsibly and use credit wisely.

Chapter 28
Insurance

Reinforcing Vocabulary

Activity A **Name** ____________________
Chapter 28 **Date** ______________ **Period** __________

Match the following terms with their correct definitions. Then write a paragraph using the chapter terms to describe a fictitious person's insurance situation.

_______ 1. A managed health care plan insurance for which members pay a set fee and receive medical care, as needed, from a participating doctor or hospital.

_______ 2. A managed health care plan in which an organization of doctors or hospitals contract with an insurance company to provide health services.

_______ 3. Insurance designed to provide financial security to the family of the insured, if that person dies.

_______ 4. A legal contract describing the rights and responsibilities of a person purchasing insurance and those of the company offering it.

_______ 5. The amount of money paid for insurance.

_______ 6. The amount a policyholder must pay before an insurance company will pay a claim.

_______ 7. Requesting payment from your insurance company for a covered loss.

_______ 8. A payout, usually annual, on money earned on whole life insurance.

_______ 9. Insurance that provides for people who become unable to work due to serious illness or injury. It allows disabled employees to receive a percentage of their incomes for an extended period of time.

_______ 10. Insurance that protects your possessions against fire, theft, or other types of loss. Property insurance also provides liability coverage in the event that someone is injured in your home.

A. deductible
B. disability insurance
C. dividend
D. health maintenance organization (HMO)
E. insurance claim
F. life insurance
G. policy
H. preferred provider organization (PPO)
I. premium
J. property insurance

____

____

____

____

____

____

Car Insurance Costs

Activity B **Name** ______________________________
Chapter 28 **Date** ________________ **Period** __________

Contact a local insurance company. Request the necessary information to complete the form below regarding automobile insurance coverage. Then choose the types of coverage you would like to have and figure your total premium. Compare your form with classmates to see if another company would offer you lower rates.

Company ______________________________

1. What are the premium costs for the following types of coverage?
   A. Bodily injury insurance ______________________________
   What is the limit of liability per person? ________________ per accident? ________________
   B. Property damage insurance ______________________________
   What is the limit of liability per accident? ______________________________
   C. Collision insurance ______________________________

What deductibles are available? ______________________________

2. What other types of auto coverage are available and what is the cost for each type?
   A. ______________________________
   B. ______________________________
   C. ______________________________
3. What discounts are available and what is the value of each?
   A. ______________________________
   B. ______________________________
   C. ______________________________

List the types of automobile coverage you would buy and the cost for each type.

	Coverage	**Cost**
A.	______________________	__________
B.	______________________	__________
C.	______________________	__________
D.	______________________	__________
E.	______________________	__________
	Total	__________

List the discounts for which you would qualify and the value of each discount.

	Discount	**Value**
A.	______________________	__________
B.	______________________	__________
	Total	__________

Subtract the total value of the discounts from the total cost of the insurance. What is your total premium?

____

Personal Property Inventory

Activity C | **Name** ______________________
Chapter 28 | **Date** ____________ **Period** ________

Keeping a current record of your property will help you in reporting lost or stolen property. Use this form to take inventory of your property.

Item Description (Include brand name, model #, and/or serial # when possible.)	Date of Purchase	Purchase Price and Tax	Place of Purchase

Understanding Insurance

Activity D
Chapter 28

Name ______________________
Date ______________ **Period** __________

Answer the following questions to show your understanding of the concepts presented in the chapter.

1. What is the difference between the insurer and the insured? ______________________

2. What type of automobile insurance protects you against the claims of other people? ______________________

3. What type of automobile insurance protects you against court actions or claims for injuries to other people? ______________________

4. What type of automobile insurance protects other people's property against damage that you cause? ______________________

5. What type of automobile insurance pays for repairs to your car even if you are at fault? ______________________

6. Why might a person decide not to carry collision insurance on his or her automobile? ______________________

7. Name three costs besides hospital stays and examinations by physicians that may be covered under health insurance. ______________________

8. What is an advantage of having group health insurance rather than buying health insurance on your own? ______________________

9. What is a *beneficiary*? ______________________

10. What is *cash value*? ______________________

11. What is an advantage of term life insurance over whole life insurance? ______________________

12. Compared with a married person, does a single person need more or less life insurance? ______________________

13. Who receives benefits under disability insurance? ______________________

14. What is the purpose of property insurance? ______________________

15. What type of property insurance pays the full cost of new items? ______________________

16. How can a personal property inventory be helpful to a renter or homeowner? ______________________

17. Give an example of a situation in which you would need to file a claim. ______________________

Chapter 29
A Place to Live

Reinforcing Vocabulary

Activity A Name ______________________________
Chapter 29 Date ____________ Period ____________

Complete the following definitions by writing the missing term(s) in the preceding blanks.

furnished apartment
lease
real estate
rental agency
roommate
security deposit
unfurnished apartment
verbal agreement

______________________ 1. Store clearances and garage sales are good places to shop for low-cost items needed in a(n) _____ _____.

______________________ 2. An apartment owner will use a tenant's _____ _____ to make necessary repairs due to damage caused by the tenant.

______________________ 3. A(n) _____ explains in writing the rights and responsibilities of the tenant and the owner.

______________________ 4. Living with a(n) _____ is an alternative to living at home or living alone.

______________________ 5. A(n) _____ _____ will refer a person to available apartments for a fee.

______________________ 6. A tenant who rents a(n) _____ _____ does not need to supply any of his or her own furniture.

______________________ 7. When a tenant and an owner agree on a rental arrangement without putting anything in writing, they make a(n) _____ _____.

______________________ 8. Although most _____ _____ agencies handle the buying and selling of houses, some also handle rental properties.

Apartment Search

Activity B **Name** ______________________________
Chapter 29 **Date** _______________ **Period** __________

Using the classified section of the newspaper or the Internet, gather information about one furnished and two unfurnished apartments to complete the chart below. Then answer the questions that follow.

	Furnished Apartment	Unfurnished Apartment A	Unfurnished Apartment B
Address			
Number of bedrooms			
Monthly rent			
Utilities included in the rent			
Security deposit required			
Length of lease			
Amount of storage space			
On-site parking			
Nearby public transportation			
On-site laundry facilities			

Which of the three apartments you investigated would you most like to rent? Explain.

____

____

Which of the three apartments you investigated would you least like to rent? Explain.

____

____

____

Would you rather rent a furnished or an unfurnished apartment? Explain.

____

____

Would you rather live alone or share an apartment with a roommate? Explain.

____

Furnishing an Apartment

Activity C
Chapter 29

Name ______________________________
Date ________________ **Period** __________

In the chart below, list all the furnishings you would need if you moved into an unfurnished apartment. Don't forget to include linens, dishes, cookware, cleaning supplies, and other household items. For each item listed, check the appropriate column to indicate whether you would borrow it or receive it as a gift, buy it used, or buy it new. Use the classified ads in your newspaper to estimate prices of the used items you plan to buy. Use store ads, catalogs, or the Internet to estimate prices of the new items you plan to buy. Then add the total of your planned purchases.

Item	Borrow/ Gift	Buy Used	Buy New	Estimated Price
Total:				

Housing Costs

Activity D
Chapter 29

Name ______________________________
Date ____________________ **Period** ____________

Complete this activity to help you estimate the cost of moving into an apartment.

1. Assume you will rent one of the unfurnished apartments you investigated in Activity B. What is your monthly rent? ______________________________

2. For all utilities not included in the rent, estimate their typical monthly bills. Ask the owner of the apartment or your local utility companies for estimates. Record all expenses that would apply to you.

   Electric company monthly bill ____________________

   Gas company monthly bill ____________________

   Water company monthly bill ____________________

   Telephone company monthly bill ____________________

   Total: ____________________

3. Add the totals from items 1 and 2.

   ____________________ + ____________________ = ____________________

4. Some guidelines suggest limiting your rent and utility costs to one-third of your take-home pay. Using this guideline, what would your take-home pay need to be if you were living in this apartment?

   ____

5. Some additional expenses occur when you first move into an apartment. Contact the apartment owner and your local utility companies to enter all expenses that would apply to you.

   Credit check by apartment owner ____________________

   Security deposit for apartment ____________________

   Electric company deposit ____________________

   Gas company deposit ____________________

   Water company deposit ____________________

   Telephone company deposit ____________________

   Furnishings (from Activity C) ____________________

   Total: ____________________

6. List other items you would need to pay for if you were living in an apartment (food, laundry, transportation or gasoline, insurance, etc.). ______________________________

   ____

   ____

7. After having completed the above, what have you determined about the cost of independent living?

   ____

   ____

8. What could you do to reduce some of your expenses? ______________________________

   ____

   ____

Chapter 30
Transportation

Reinforcing Vocabulary

Activity A
Chapter 30

Name ______________________________
Date ____________________ **Period** ____________

Match the following terms with their correct definitions. In the space below, write a brief story about someone traveling to work. Correctly use all the terms in the story.

_______ 1. A list of the expected arrival and departure times and locations for buses, trains, subways, and airplanes.
_______ 2. A group of people who take turns driving to a common location or area.
_______ 3. Transportation, such as buses or trains, used routinely by the general public.
_______ 4. To change from one bus or train route to another in order to get to the right place.
_______ 5. An organization that operates a transportation system.

A. car pool
B. carrier
C. mass transportation
D. schedule
E. transfer

Reading a Bus Schedule

Activity B **Name** ______________________________
Chapter 30 **Date** ________________ **Period** __________

Use the bus schedule on the next page to answer the questions below.

1. What telephone number would you use to find out what time you could catch a bus at the Broad Street stop? ______________________________
2. What telephone number would you use to complain about a rude bus driver? ______________
3. On what holidays does this schedule operate? ______________________________
____
4. On what days of the week does this schedule not operate? ______________________________
____
5. What five activities are prohibited on the bus? ______________________________
____
____
6. Can passengers expect to get change from the bus driver? Explain. ______________________________
____
____
7. Approximately how many minutes is the ride from Green Street to Spring Road? ______________
8. On what bus line is the Park Avenue stop? ______________________________
9. What does the O symbol mean? ______________________________
10. Suppose you arrive at Industry Park at 5:50 P.M. on the Downtown Express. How long will you have to wait at the stop for a North Loop bus to arrive? ______________________________
11. Which bus lines stop at Capitol Towers? ______________________________
12. What time does the first Downtown Express bus arrive at Industry Park? ______________
13. What time does the last bus of the day arrive at Glenwood Plaza, and which bus line is it? __________
____
14. How would you get from Carson Parkway to Glenwood Plaza? ______________________________
15. Suppose you live near the Center Street stop and have an appointment on Oak Street at 9:30 A.M. Which buses on which lines would you use to get there? ______________________________
____
____
16. Name all the stops on the Center/Arbor line. ______________________________
____
____
____

RAPID BUS WEEKDAY RUSH	North Loop Line originates Columbus Blvd. 7:20 A.M.	Downtown Express originates Highland Rd. 7:45 A.M.	Center/Arbor Line originates Center St. 7:30 A.M.
Industry Park	7:55 A.M. 8:25 A.M. 8:55 A.M. 4:55 P.M. 5:25 P.M. 5:55 P.M.	7:50 A.M. 8:20 A.M. 8:50 A.M. 4:50 P.M. 5:20 P.M. 5:50 P.M.	______ ______ ______ ______ ______ ______
Fountain Square	7:35 A.M. 8:05 A.M. 8:35 A.M. 4:35 P.M. 5:05 P.M. 5:35 P.M.	______ ______ ______ ______ ______ ______	7:45 A.M. 8:45 A.M. 9:45 A.M. 6:15 P.M. 7:15 P.M. 8:15 P.M.
Capitol Towers	7:40 A.M. 8:10 A.M. 8:40 A.M. 4:40 P.M. 5:10 P.M. 5:40 P.M.	8:10 A.M. 8:40 A.M. 9:10 A.M. 5:10 P.M. 5:40 P.M. 6:10 P.M.	______ ______ ______ ______ ______ ______
Glenwood Plaza	______ ______ ______ ______ ______ ______	8:15 A.M. 8:45 A.M. 9:15 A.M. 5:15 P.M. 5:45 P.M. 6:15 P.M.	7:55 A.M. 8:55 A.M. 9:55 A.M. 6:25 P.M. 7:25 P.M. 8:25 P.M.

This schedule operates Monday through Friday, including Presidents' Day, Columbus Day, and Veterans' Day.

This schedule does not operate Saturdays, Sundays, or the following holidays: New Year's Day, Memorial Day, Independence Day, Labor Day, Thanksgiving, and Christmas.

For schedule information, call 555-TRIP.
For customer service, call 555-HELP.

Passengers must have exact fare. No eating, drinking, smoking, littering, or loud radio playing allowed on RAPID buses.

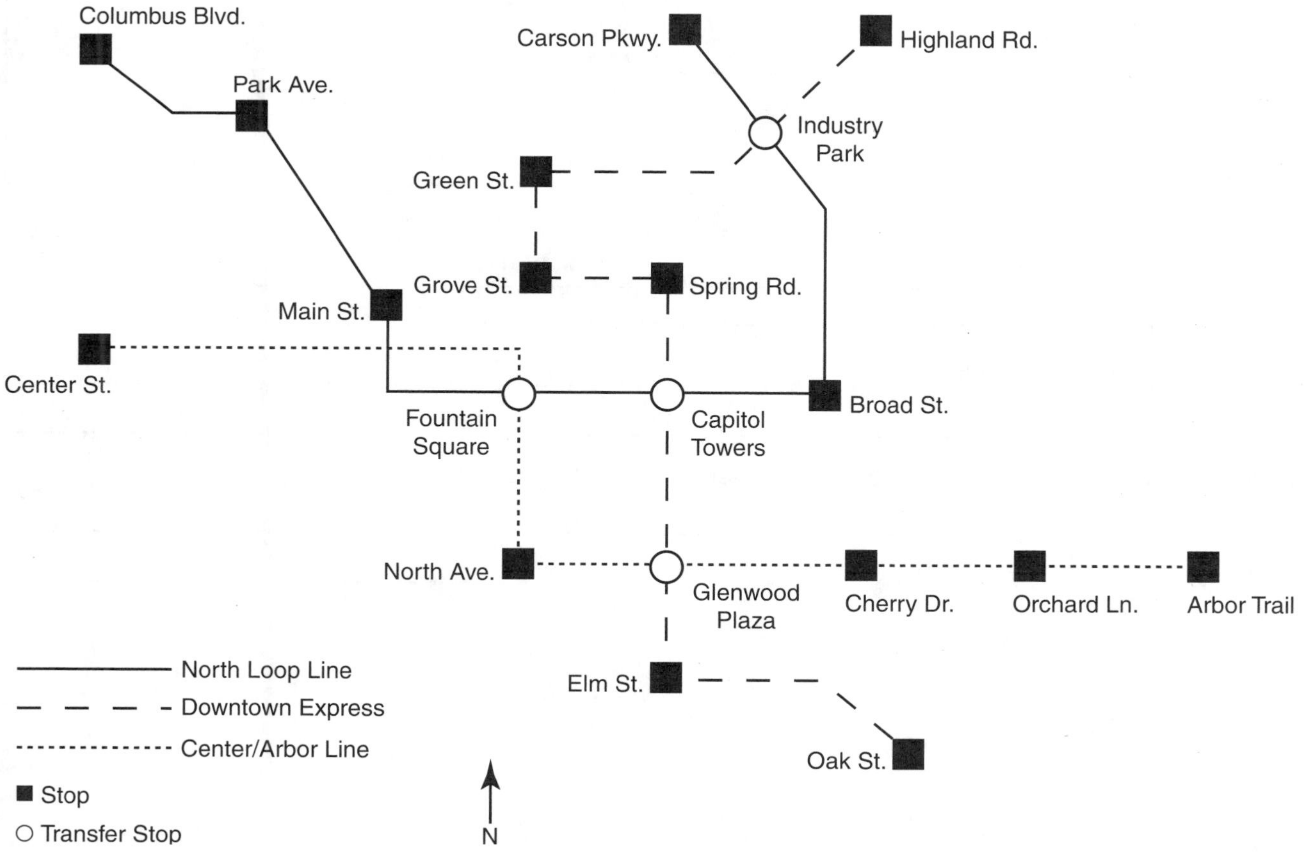

Transportation Comparison

Activity C
Chapter 30

Name ______________________
Date ______________ **Period** __________

Complete the chart to express your view of the advantages and disadvantages of various types of transportation. Then answer the questions that follow.

	Advantages	**Disadvantages**
Self-powered transportation Walking		
Riding a bicycle		
Automobile transportation Drive yourself		
Car pool		
Mass transportation Buses		
Trains and subways		
Airplanes		

1. Which type of transportation would you most likely use to get to work? Explain.______________________
____
2. Under what circumstances might you choose another type of transportation? ______________________
____
____
3. Which type of transportation would you least likely use to get to work? Explain.______________________
____
____

Chapter 31
Being a Responsible Citizen

Reinforcing Vocabulary

Activity A
Chapter 31

Name ____________________
Date ____________ **Period** ________

Match the following terms with their correct definitions. Then write a paragraph using the chapter terms to describe what it means to be a responsible citizen.

_____ 1. The exclusive possession and control of a product or service.
_____ 2. Two or more parties acting independently to offer the most favorable product or terms.
_____ 3. The right to complain and receive an appropriate response.
_____ 4. A person who owes allegiance to a government.
_____ 5. To submit one's name to the official list of citizens eligible to vote in elections.
_____ 6. A proposed law.
_____ 7. Laws that define a person's rights in relation to other people.
_____ 8. Laws that define a person's rights in relation to government.

A. bill
B. citizen
C. civil laws
D. competition
E. monopoly
F. public laws
G. recourse
H. register

Voters' Survey

Activity B
Chapter 31

Name ______________________
Date ______________ **Period** __________

Survey five adults about their voting habits and opinions. Record their responses in the chart provided. Compile your results with those of your classmates. Write an article for your school or local newspaper reporting your findings.

1. What is your sex?
2. What is your age? A. 18 to 25 B. 26 to 40 C. 41 to 65 D. over 65
3. Are you registered to vote? (*Yes* or *No*)
4. How often do you vote?
   A. in most national, state, and local elections
   B. only in national elections
   C. never
5. How important is it for citizens to exercise their right to vote?
   A. very important
   B. somewhat important
   C. somewhat unimportant
   D. not important
6. What do you think is the most common reason some citizens do not vote?
   A. They are not familiar with the candidates and/or issues.
   B. They do not care about the results of the election.
   C. They do not feel their individual votes make a difference.
   D. They are too busy.
   E. (Write other reasons in the chart.)
7. Do you know the names of your elected officials? (*Yes* or *No*)
8. Do you feel you understand how laws are made? (*Yes* or *No*)

Survey Responses

Question	Person 1	Person 2	Person 3	Person 4	Person 5
1.					
2.					
3.					
4.					
5.					
6.					
7.					
8.					

Classroom Council

Activity C
Chapter 31

Name ______________________
Date ____________ **Period** ________

Hold a classroom election to elect seven students to serve as members of a classroom council—the governing body of your classroom. Complete the items below to pass a law in your classroom.

1. Write a law that you would like to propose to the citizens of your classroom. Be sure to choose the wording of your bill carefully. Citizens may not vote for bills that are not clear and specific.

   ____

   ____

2. List your reasons for wanting the law.

   A. ____

   B. ____

   C. ____

3. You must be prepared to defend your bill against arguments by citizens who do not support it. List two reasons you think some may oppose the bill and provide a response to each.

   A. Reason: ____

   ____

   Response: ____

   ____

   B. Reason: ____

   ____

   Response: ____

   ____

4. If you are not an elected council member, temporarily replace one of the students who is. Now that you have written your bill and prepared for the debate, present it to the class. Give citizens in your class time to debate the bill. List any new points that are mentioned during the debate.

   A. Points in favor: ____

   ____

   B. Arguments against: ____

   ____

5. Revise the wording of your bill based on comments made during the debate.

   ____

   ____

6. Present your revised bill to the class. After completing any further discussion, have the council vote on your bill. What were the results of the vote?

   (number) ________ votes for the bill

   (number) ________ votes against the bill

7. Based on this experience, what would you do differently if you were proposing this bill again?

   ____

   ____

Legal Advice

Activity D **Name** ______________________________
Chapter 31 **Date** ____________________ **Period** ____________

Invite a lawyer, law student, or legal aide to class or interview one. Find out the answers to the questions below.

1. What are the most common reasons people seek the advice of a lawyer? ____________________
____
2. What is the best way to find a lawyer? ____________________
____
3. Are there any drawbacks to finding a lawyer through the Yellow Pages? ____________________
____
4. How useful is a state legal association in helping someone find a lawyer? ____________________
____
5. In what types of legal services do you specialize? ____________________
____
6. How important is it to choose a lawyer who is qualified to deal with a particular type of legal problem? Why is it important? ____________________
____
7. On the average, how much do legal services cost? ____________________
8. Where can someone who is unable to afford a lawyer get legal help? ____________________
9. How adequate are free legal services provided by a public service agency? ____________________
____
10. What problems could arise if a person fails to consult a lawyer in each of the following situations?
    A. when buying a house ____________________
    ____
    B. when getting a divorce ____________________
    ____
    C. when breaking a lease ____________________
    ____
    D. after receiving a summons or subpoena ____________________
    ____
    E. after being arrested ____________________
    ____
    F. when preparing a will ____________________
    ____
    G. when settling an estate ____________________
    ____
    H. when trying to resolve a consumer problem ____________________
    ____

Writing a Complaint Letter

Activity E
Chapter 31

Name ________________________
Date ______________ **Period** __________

Write a complaint letter about one of the following consumer problems. Create any missing details. Be sure to use proper business letter format as shown in the text.

Problem #1: You bought a tube of Brite White toothpaste. The label on the toothpaste claimed that your teeth would be noticeably whiter after using the toothpaste for just one week. You've been using the toothpaste for 10 days and you still haven't noticed a difference.

Problem #2: You bought Old Favorites Jean Softener, a kit designed to give new blue jeans an old, faded look. You followed the directions on the package exactly. When you removed your jeans from the solution, they fell apart at the seams.

Problem #3: You bought a Plushy Puppy stuffed toy for your nephew's birthday. While wrapping it, one of the eyes fell off. You noticed that the eye had a sharp point on it. You are concerned that your nephew could have been injured if he had been playing with the toy.

Citizen Awareness

Activity F Name ______________________

Chapter 31 Date ____________ Period ________

Read the following statements about topics from the chapter. Circle *T* if the statement is true or *F* if the statement is false.

T F 1. Any citizen of the United States who is at least 21 years old has the right to vote.
T F 2. Citizens are responsible for making laws.
T F 3. In order to vote, a citizen must register.
T F 4. Citizens can register to vote at most lawyers' offices.
T F 5. Federal laws are made by the United States Congress.
T F 6. A debate is the discussion of a proposed law by members of the legislature.
T F 7. Citizens may vote to accept a proposition, causing it to become a law.
T F 8. Local bills may be printed in the newspaper before being brought to a vote at town council meetings.
T F 9. The laws in the United States are divided into two categories—criminal laws and international laws.
T F 10. Civil laws relate to cases involving such issues as contracts, inheritances, and the business of corporations.
T F 11. Presidents, governors, and mayors are members of the executive branches of federal, state, and local governments, respectively.
T F 12. Most lawyers handle all types of cases, so any lawyer could deal with any legal problems a person might have.
T F 13. A person who is unable to afford a lawyer has no way to receive help with a legal problem.
T F 14. The only time a person needs a lawyer is if he or she is arrested.
T F 15. In a free enterprise system, both citizens and businesses have rights and responsibilities.
T F 16. Manufacturers can legally make any claims they wish on the labels of their products, whether or not they are true.
T F 17. Monopolies are against the law.
T F 18. Consumers have a responsibility to report products they find to be unsafe.
T F 19. Writing letters to the Better Business Bureau is the first step in correcting consumer problems.
T F 20. Generally, the BBB and a government agency will not handle the same complaint at the same time.